The Divine Symphony

An Exordium to the Theology of the Catholic Mass

The Divine Symphony

An Exordium to the Theology of the Catholic Mass

David L. Gray

Saint Dominic's Media

Belleville, Illinois

Published by:
Saint Dominic's Media, Inc.
P.O. Box 8225
Belleville, IL 62222

www.saintdominicsmedia.com

Cover Design by:
Saudia Y. Mills

Printed in the United States of America

19 29 21 22 23 24 25   8 7 6 5 4 3 2

BISAC Category:
Religion / Christian Rituals & Practice / Worship & Liturgy

ISBN-13: 978-1-7321784-0-3 (Paperback)
ISBN-13: 978-1-7321784-1-0 (Hardback)
ISBN-13: 978-1-7321784-2-7 (E-book)

For the People of God

To my wife Felicia, and my daughters
Daeleon, Daeja, Daerielle, and Olivia.

In sincere gratitude to Benedict XVI, great teacher,
and my inspiration in becoming and being Catholic

Contents

Exordium to the Introductory Rite
> Subjects: the Introductory Rite as a type of sonata, Why God reveals Himself, God's silent Presence, sacred space, **the Entrance and Procession**, the purpose of liturgical music, the posture of standing, versus Populum, the Sign of the Cross, opening greetings, periodic phrasing (call and response), Babel resolved by the Admirable Exchange, **the Penitential Rite to the Collect**, the Confiteor, sacramental absolution, Kyrie Eleison, the Gloria in Excelsis Deo, the Collect

Exordium to the Liturgy of the Word
> Subjects: the relationship between the Liturgy of the Word and the Liturgy of the Eucharist, early attestation to the Liturgy of the Word, the four Presences of God at the Mass, the posture of sitting, the character of the liturgical readings, **the Biblical readings**, the First reading, the Psalms, the Second reading, the Gospel reading, the posture of standing, **the Homily**, early attestation to the Homily, purpose of the Homily, **the Creed, the Universal Prayer**, early attestation to the Universal Prayer, the character of intercessory prayer

Contents

Proem

What is the Divine Symphony? The *Ite, Missa est* is a Divine Symphony, written by the People of God, and inspired by the Divine Composer. The purpose of the Divine Symphony is to communicate to God's People the story of the memorial sacrifice of His Beloved and Begotten Son. The Divine Symphony intends to fill us with all that we need to be like Christ Jesus and to serve Him fully so that we will be happy with Him in this life and the next.

I love the classical symphony orchestra. Although, it must be stated that I was never a music major. My Bachelor of Science degree is in Business Administration, and my Master of Arts degree is in Theology. I play the trumpet, but I have not played in a band since tenth grade. That is to say that, I am far out of my academic and practicing depth when it comes to music theory and history, but my love for it has, over the years, caused me to study it and grow in some knowledge of it. After my conversion to Catholicism, I began to develop more profound understanding and love of the Mass, and I started to imagine these two things together. I began to see the classical form of the symphony orchestra in the Mass and the Mass in some of the classical compositions. I saw The Divine Symphony!

While no analogy is perfect, and they all eventually fall apart, the basic idea is that a symphony is a sentence (*satz* in German); a series of sentences called movements that are related to one another and come together to form one paragraph. In the classical symphony, there were four of these movements, freestanding; one ending before the next one begins after a pause, but all four of them thematically related to the other to communicate one story. Similarly, the Mass is like a paragraph that has been composed to tell a story in four movements (Opening Rite, Rite of the Liturgy of the Word, Rite of the Liturgy of the Eucharist, and the Closing Rite). While there are many distinctions between the classical symphony and the Divine Symphony, as an analogy it seems to me to be a much closer fit than some of the others.

In addition to the analogy, another essential feature of this exordium is the cursory inclusion and comparison of the various liturgical expressions of the memorial sacrifice. When Pope Pius V officially promulgated the Tridentine Liturgy on July 14, 1570, through his Apostolic Constitution, *Quo Primum*, he stated that:

> This new rite alone is to be used unless approval of the practice of saying Mass differently was given at the very time of the institution and confirmation of the church by Apostolic See at least 200 years ago, or unless there has prevailed a custom of a similar kind which has been continuously followed for a period of not less than 200 years, in which most cases We in no wise rescind their above-mentioned prerogative or custom.

Still today, many of these Latin rites of the *Ite, Missa est* such as the Lyonensis, Bracarensis, Cartussiensis, Carmelitanus, Ambrosianus, and the Mozarabicus are being celebrated in the Latin language throughout the world. In the East, we find the Liturgy of Saint James and the Liturgy of Saint John Chrysostom being practiced by the Orthodox Churches (including those in union with Rome), the Liturgy of Saint Basil, bishop of Caesarea, the Liturgy of Saint Cyril the 24th Patriarch of the Coptic Orthodox Church, and Liturgy of Saint Gregory of Nazianzus being practiced by the Coptic Orthodox Church, and the Liturgy of Saint Mark being worked by a small number of Russian and Greek Orthodox communities.

In this exordium to the theology of the memorial sacrifice, the post-Second Vatican Council Novus Ordo Rite is primarily used as the liturgical outline, but I have also incorporated for comparisons, contrasts, and more in-depth expositions of the mystery, parts of some of the aforementioned liturgies. In doing so, the hope is that the reader might: (1) See how these various expressions of the memorial sacrifice are all praying and confessing the same things, due in part to the cross-pollination of liturgical expression in the early centuries of the Church; thereby demonstrating how it is the Holy Spirit who inspires the unity of liturgy; and (2) See how truly the Novus Ordo Rite is connected to the older rites. Therefore, this exordium hereby suffices as my complete response to those who reject the Novus Ordo Rite on the grounds of authority and history. This work is also my partial and non-defensive response to those who have qualms with the Novus Ordo Rite on the grounds of orientation and aesthetics.

It is always true, that the deeper you know something, the more you will understand how to use it or how valuable it is or can be to you. The more valuable a thing is to you, the better you will grow in appreciation of it; and, perhaps, even desire and love it more deeply. Apply those sayings to anything; whether it be an inanimate object or a person; the more time you spend studying that thing, the more you will discover about it, and in finding its purpose and value, you will discover what positive or negative impact it has or can have on your life.

In the instant case, through our neglect in teaching the mysteries of the liturgy, we have nurtured generations of People who do not rightly know, understand, value, appreciate, or love the Mass. Then when we did try to teach liturgy, we taught it poorly. We taught it as a list of things we say, things the Priest says, times we stand, times we kneel, things we do, and things we don't do. Ironically, we watered down the liturgy to be an itemized menu, and then wondered how we ended up with 'à la carte menu Catholics' who unscrupulously pick and choose what teachings they want to believe, and what teachings they do not. Now, because they do not know the Mass, they do not love it, and because they do not love it, they do not reverently pray it.

Our lack of knowing, loving, and reverently praying the Mass has caused great harm in the world. For, what God has given us in the liturgy to share His peace and to inspire order in the world, has, through our disabilities, only caused more division.

Our inability to communicate the true beauty of our highest form of prayer has led to poor evangelization. We have created a whole system of trying to teach the faith through defending it; that is, by telling people Catholics are right because Protestants are wrong. Even though Protestantism has nothing, whatsoever, true to say outside of the Catholic Church, for some strange reason we thought that the dim-light of their teaching could help us project the great light. Because we did not understand the liturgy well enough to teach through it, we created the modern system of apologetics, which is unable to teach its mysteries positively. On the contrary, there is no more excellent or more effective way to understand what the Church teaches and why She teaches it than through Her memorial sacrifice.

Furthermore, our inability to communicate the real beauty of our highest form of prayer has led to elitism and prejudice within the Church; Catholics thinking that their expression of the memorial sacrifice being better, or even more efficacious than other rites – as if there is more of Jesus, the Holy Eucharist, at the Tridentine Mass than there is at the Novus Ordo, or that there is more of Jesus at the Byzantine Divine Liturgy than there is at the Tridentine. On the contrary, as God is one, so is His memorial sacrifice. As God is one, so is there only one Mass that is expressed through various liturgical traditions that are rooted in a Divinely inspired cross-pollination with each other, especially for the first seven centuries of the Church.

Therefore, how can we recover the orthodoxy? How can we inspire the People to know, love, and reverently pray the Mass? We can accomplish that by reclaiming our theology and reframing what we believe and why we believe it, through the essential life-giving act of God, given to us throughout the covenants and found in the memorial Passover sacrifice; first instituted as a perpetual command before the exodus, and again before the Crucifixion, and now in perpetual memorial through the Divine Symphony.

For far too long, and in vain, have we tried to teach what is true outside of what is this central truth and central liturgical expression of our faith. We have danced outside of the ballroom and with a partner who is not ours, swam on dry land without a bathing suit, and performed a play far from the stage and lights and without an audience.

I wrote this book to contribute to that idea of recapturing our theology and framing it around the central truth of our faith. My hope is that this book inspires you, with the prose of theological song and theory, to know, love, and reverently pray the Mass. For, when you know the Mass, you truly know that Jesus the Christ loves you and that He is there for you. Be entirely dependent on Him for everything!

How to Use

Allow the prose of this exordium of the memorial sacrifice to accompany your memory as you participate in the liturgy of the Church. Also, allow it to serve as one of your guides to study more deeply the Divine mysteries of the sacred liturgy.

The First Movement
of
The Divine Symphony

EXORDIUM TO THE INTRODUCTORY RITES

Whether through the edible Word, the written Word, the ordained Priest *in Persona Christi*, or the prayers of the royal priesthood, during every movement and in every subject, the memorial sacrifice is simultaneously revealing both the salvific work and the immediate Presence of God to His People. To initiate such a magnanimous proposal, 'the Introductory Rite' offers that very first taste and melodic key in the historical, dramatic, and revelatory encounter between God and His People in the Divine Symphony called the *Ite, Missa est*.

If there is one first thing to know about God, it would be to know that He is tripping over Himself to reveal to us His love and His desire to commune eternally with His People and that He has never and will never stop revealing Himself to His creation. If you have ever had children who would do anything to get your attention, or if you have ever been courted by someone who goes to extreme measures to woo you into their life, you have seen just a mere shadow of a tiny glimpse of God working to get your attention, by continually revealing His love and His desires for you.

The reason why we see in the Scriptures and witness in the Christian experience, God going through such extraordinary measures to reveal Himself to His People, is because God's very nature is love,[1] and a principal property of the nature of love is an undying desire to make itself known. It is true, love can never be kept a secret, and Jesus Christ, God from God, is the fullness and the perfect manifestation of His Father's revealed love for us. For this reason, the Mass itself is Love, because the Church, the Body of Christ, participating in the Divine nature of God, through the memorial sacrifice, calls God's People to consume and to be filled and strengthen by that very same nature.

Beyond the natural necessity of Divine love, there are six other reasons why God reveals Himself. The first is so that we might know Him; second, so that we might follow Him; third, so that we might become His disciples; fourth, so that we might know the Truth; fifth, so that we might be free;[2] and sixth, so that we might not ever depart from Him.[3]

The great beauty of the Divine Symphony is that it is so ordered to accomplish this six-fold purpose of God's desire to reveal Himself to us. That is, by participating in the Mass we grow in knowing God through hearing the written word and through the lived experience of the communion of saints. Through this knowledge and the gift of faith from the Holy Spirit, we are inspired to follow God wherever He is, and through Catholic attention and intention, we become His disciples by sitting at His feet, and by adoring His Eucharistic Presence. Then, it is through that faithful and intentional discipleship that we are drawn deeper into the Truth (i.e., Jesus Christ) that He has revealed through His Church, and as we begin to live in that Truth, the shackles of sin and worldly attachments start falling off. To be free is not to

---

[1] Cf. 1 Jn. 4:8.
[2] Cf. Jn. 8:31-32.
[3] Cf. Jn. 15.

be free from anything, but, instead, it is to be free to love in, with, and through the source and nature of love, which is the Holy Trinity. In this way, the Mass conducts us down the path to true freedom.

The Introductory rites of the Tridentine and Novus Ordo Mass consists of the Entrance, Greeting, Penitential Act, Glory to God, and the Collect. These five sections in the first movement of the Divine Symphony are interrelated not in terms of content or structure, but by pure character and purpose, which intends to prepare us to worthily and most abundantly receive the graces of God through the Liturgy of the Word and the Liturgy of the Eucharist. As John the Baptist prepared the way for the Lord; similarly, the goal of these sections is to prepare the way for God's People to receive the love of their Father through Christ Jesus and to make straight their path to Him, so that they might worthily receive Him.

In the classical era, symphonies often used the sonata form to structure one or more of their movements. The sonata form consisted of three main sections: exposition, development, and recapitulation. Similarly, the five parts of the Opening Rite of the Divine Symphony falls into those three sections; shifting between prayer and confession, as if they were subjects and modulations. Whereas in a classical symphony, prior to its beginning, there would be a cacophony of discordant noises coming from instruments, accompanied by the meaningless chatter and social noise of the audience. In contrast, in the Divine Symphony, prior to the exposition of the sonata, there is a prelude of intentional silence and solitude.

Every great and significant undertaking, such as this, must be prefaced by a period of preparation, strategic planning, reflection, or trial. Whether that prelude is an antechamber, or that period of testing found in the initiation rites, or the period of staging found in a military war room, or Joshua circumcising the sons of Israel at Gibeath-haaraaloth,[4] serious matters ought to never be casually or disobediently engaged. This fact is most especially true regarding the Sacraments of the Catholic Church.

"Without the silence that precedes it, speech runs the great risk of being useless chattering . . ."[5] The chatter; the noise; the cacophony; the People's careless use of words before the Divine Symphony begins, undermines the perfect use of words in the liturgy. We pretend as if whatever picayune thing we must say is worthy of this sacred space. "Whoever uses too many words will be loathed."[6] This social chatter, community greetings (which also undermines the upcoming 'Rite of Peace'), and ordinary meandering that has invaded the sacred space of far too many of our Churches prior to 'the Entrance' only occurs when the People gathered there have presupposed the Divine Symphony to be just another ordinary social event on their calendar; when they perceive it as being nothing more than just a scattered listing of things we do, of things we don't do, of words we say, of things the Priest says, of times we kneel, and times we stand, rather than it being the opportunity to progress in that very divinization that the *Ite, Missa est* promises.

On January 22, 2006, it was only my inner sense that informed me of something wholly unique and different about the space in which I intentionally sought out. For, such a perception was most undoubtedly paradoxical being that the room in which I entered was very ordinary. It was a sixteen-foot wide and twenty-four-foot-long room, constructed from cinderblock, painted with an off-white satin sheen, and covered by a solid white ceiling, which housed two rows of three lighting panels. The altar looked like any other Minwax 'cherry-stained' wooden

---

[4] Cf. Josh. 5:3.
[5] Sarah, Robert, Diat, Nicholas. *The Power of Silence: Again the Dictatorship of Noise*. Ignatius Press. San Francisco. 2016. 34.
[6] Sir. 20:8.

box on wheels, and in the corner next to it was a steely-brown metal cabinet, which has certainly seen better days, but contained the vestments for the Priest, unconsecrated hosts, the chalice, paten, ciborium, cruet, decanter, candles, and missals. There were six pews (without kneelers) in this space. Not nearly matching the wood stain of the altar, they looked as if they were once used for Protestant gatherings in some other room in the prison. Opposite of the altar was a long window made from a transparent acrylic so that the corrections officers could spy in.

Altar and pews aside; I pondered on why did this room, which looked like every other room in the prison, where having the sense of something being foreboding was much more common than having the sense of space being sacred, gave me the perception of being otherworldly? It felt otherworldly because it exuded a clear and distinguishing character, which was wholly unlike any other space I had known before. Even in a prison, I found this sacred space, filled with holy objects and holy People; all of whom spoke of their heavenly disposition through silence.

It was their practice of intentional silence that immediately captivated the attention of my imagination. The noise of Protestant gatherings . . . the music, the chatter, the noise - all of which were imperfectly able to hold my senses captive, but never able to captivate my imagination that was reaching for God. Moreover, the Protestant gatherings were no different than what I had found in the noise of the world . . . the music, the chatter, the noise - all of which are imperfectly able to distract or tempt my senses, but never able to focus my imaginative searching for God.

Regarding the times that sacred silence is to be observed at the designed times, the *General Instruction of the Roman Missal* offers:

> Even before the celebration itself, it is a praiseworthy practice for silence to be observed in the church, in the sacristy, in the vesting room,

and in adjacent areas, so that all may dispose themselves to carry out the sacred celebration in a devout and fitting manner.[7]

Indeed, the Divine Symphony must begin in such a place of solitude and with the practice of intentional silence because it is in this type of set-apart space and with such a mirroring of internal disposition that we were created to find our Creator. Into this state of solitude and disposition of silence, God calls each of us to discover the path to growing more rooted in knowledge and love of Him who knew and loved us when we were but silent in His foreknowledge of us.

The examples that *Luke* sets forth of Christ Jesus praying in a set-apart space of silence and solitude finds the Lord praying in a desert,[8] a mountain,[9] alone with His disciples,[10] and in a "certain place."[11] Contained within Jesus' example is the paradox of prayer being a place of retreat. Why must we retreat into prayer to God if God is omnipresent? The answer to that question begins with a question like this; why did God have to create us to love us? Certainly, God could have just as perfectly loved the image of us that was contained within Him. On the contrary, communion with the one whom we love demands intentionality towards communion. Guided by the intention and desire to meet God, prayer becomes greater than being merely a 'thing' we do; rather, it becomes a state of being truly alive in God. In this way, the physical act of 'going' to pray in silence and solitude is joined with the mental and spiritual act of praying and being in prayer.

---

[7] *GIRM*, Chapter II, 45.
[8] Cf. Lk. 5:12-16.
[9] Cf. Lk. 6:9-12, 9:28-35; 22:9-35.
[10] Cf. Lk. 8:18-20.
[11] Cf. Lk. 11:1-13.

Oftentimes an engaged couple will express to their pastor their desire for an outdoor wedding; perhaps to be on some scenic white-sand beach or at an isolated red farmhouse or at some other extraordinary unique, picturesque, memorable, and altogether cliché location. To which a well-informed pastor would respond by saying something about the Sacrament of Holy Matrimony is rightly consecrated in the House of God. To which the bride, who has desired a cliché outdoor wedding ceremony her entire life up to this point will retort, 'But God is everywhere.' Indeed, the bride is myopically correct in exclaiming God's omnipresence, but even He commanded what materials, furnishings, and ornaments Moses should adorn His Temple with. Certainly, God knows He's omnipresent, yet, despite His self-awareness and omnipresence, He still deigns for spaces be set-apart for humans to worship, adore, and uniquely encounter Him. "In my Father's house are many rooms; if it were not so, would I have told you that I go to prepare a place for you?"[12] The mental and spiritual act of intentionally 'going' to pray and confess the Mass in the house of God - the set-apart and sacred space on Earth, most perfectly equips the Christian for their intentional pilgrimage to that room Christ Jesus has prepared for them in Heaven.

We are silent in those moments before the memorial sacrifice begins; prior to 'The Entrance' processional, both, because we recognize that this set-apart space indeed is a state of solitude and because we wait in prayerful adoration of the God whose nature is silence.

The notion of the Mass being a state of solitude at first seems contradictory to reality. For, how can I be all alone, isolated, secluded, and solitary while I am gathered together with the People of God? Perhaps the Gothic and Romanesque styles of architecture captured this truth better than then modern cavernous and

---

[12] Jn. 14:2.

commercial designs of many Catholic Churches today. The former structures made us feel small, little and distant from God. They humbled the greatest of us before the awesome Presence of the *I Am*. Though I am surrounded by the many; before God, I am secluded, yet alone with Him. It is within this state of solitude, where we feel an immense distance and approaching intimacy with God that we are most silent.

This silence is not to be confused with quiet, which is merely concerned with noise and the sense of hearing. In the spiritual sense, these two words, quiet and silence, are not synonymous. On the contrary, there is an inner state of solitude where man can dwell in silence without regard to the audible noises of the world. It was in this state that Elijah met God at Mount Horeb; not in the wind, nor the earthquake, not in the fire, but in a still small voice that permeated through them all.[13] Likewise, the memorial sacrifice is a state of solitude that we enter without regard to the distractions of the world. Here, God is found in silence because silence is an attribute genuinely belonging to His nature and being. Therefore, it belongs to the first order of the Mass to withdraw into its solitude so that we might seek, hear, and find the God's silent word and presence.

This first order of the Mass is not intended for passivity; instead, it is intended to dispose us into the disposition of active prayer. For, the highest truth and the most significant secret about the Mass is that it is an unceasing prayer and confession to God our Father. Most certainly, if all Catholics knew the Mass as prayer, perhaps there would be fewer Catholics standing with their hands in the pockets or treating such a uniquely transcendent, cosmic, and holy occasion as if it were something ordinary

---

[13] Cf. 1 Kings 19:11-12.

and routine. Indeed, if the Mass was known for what it is, the internal disposition of the People's prayers would be reflected in an outward disposition of awe-impacted reverence.

Although we have retreated into this sacred space; this state of solitude, we can no more remain here than Adam remained all-lone, or Samuel remained in the Temple, or Jesus remained in prayer away from His disciples. For us, this was merely an antechamber of initiation into the Sacramental Mysteries. Although silence is more profoundly present at this beginning cycle of the Mass, it will not entirely depart, but, rather, will deign to interrupt the Mass so that we might be drawn back again to the sheer otherness of God and humbly quake and boldly confess that we are being conformed to His image and likeness.

For what shall we pray? As with all prayers, the Mass begins in silent contemplation, which draws us into our smallness, but from which we emerge audaciously and boldly in praise and thanksgiving. It is here that the cacophony of prayers of the faithful are comingled and readied to rise united unto God like the scent of burning incense.

THE ENTRANCE, REVERENCE TO THE ALTAR, AND GREETING OF THE ASSEMBLED PEOPLE

The opening of the Divine Symphony begins here in the first movement of the Mass, which is truly an exposition of the Priest, Deacons, and People of God moving slowly to the sanctuary where our prayers and confessions will be drawn out and ready our mind, body, and soul to receive the Word of God. As an exposition at a symphony orchestra would introduce the audience to the main themes of the work. The purpose of this Divine exposition is to attune the People's mind, body, and soul to the subject of their salvation and divination.

It was years before I ever heard a choir singing or instruments playing in the sacred space, and I was wholly disturbed at my first hearing, having been so used to there being silence throughout the memorial sacrifice. In fact, I am still wholly disturbed by some of our musical selections. Here and at other times where the choir is at liberty to offer a melody within the Divine melody, their selection should always reflect the qualities noted by Robert Cardinal Sarah, who wrote, "Here music, by its expressive character, by its ability to convert souls, causes the human heart to vibrate in union with God's heart. Here music rediscovers its sacredness and Divine origin."[14] That is, the goal of liturgical music is not to entertain, make happy, or stir unchaste emotions. Instead, its singular goal is court the People of God deeper into His great mystery; of God becoming man, so that man might be like God.

I have prayed many Masses in our Eastern-Rite Catholic Churches; particularly those of the Maronite, Byzantine, and Melkite rites. In fact, there was a period of time in my life when I was in discernment about moving East into the Melkite Church. For a person who loves the drama of the Mass played out through ritual, song, and mystery, there is nothing more dramatic than the Eastern liturgies. I do find beauty in the Mass of Trent, and I'm in deep love with the Dominican's Missa Cantata, but my liturgical heart resonates in the East.

Primarily in the Eastern liturgies (Carthusians also never genuflect, but make a profound bow), standing or sitting are the only two whole-body prayer postures (not including hands or head lifted up), but in West, there is a third; kneeling, which will be discussed later. The tradition in the East against showing signs of humility on Sunday was first attested to by Tertullian in his *On the Crown*, from the late 2nd century, "We count fasting or kneeling in worship on the Lord's Day to be unlawful."[15] Again, in

---

[14] *The Power of Silence*, 24.
[15] Chapter 3.

On Prayer, "We, however (just as we have received) only on the day of the Lord's Resurrection ought to guard not only against kneeling but every posture and office of solicitude . . ."[16] It was also documented later in Canon XV of the *Rudder* by St. Peter of Alexandria (3rd century), and in Book II, Ch. 59 of the *Apostolic Constitutions* (4th century).

For the Latins, standing is the position of giving attention to the present matter, and when we stand in prayer, it is to give attention and a sign of awareness of Divine matters. Standing in prayer is the first disposition we assume after coming out of our state of solitude because it signals our intention and readiness to prepare to make a sacrifice acceptable to the Lord.

To open a broader dialogue so that we might more deeply explore the richness of 'The Entrance' or the Divine exposition, it may be helpful to first visit two entrances in sacred Scripture that are abundantly grander than all the others and most closely prefigure this part of the memorial sacrifice. Then we will turn to the most solemn of all entrances in the history of mankind.

The first narrative occurs at *2 Samuel* 6 after King David had retrieved the Ark of God (Covenant) from the house of Obed-edom, where it had been for the three months and, through the Lord, had been a tremendous blessing for Obed-edom and his household. King David knew that the Ark would prove to be an awesome blessing to his household as well. "So David went and brought up the ark of God from the house of Obed-edom to the city of David with rejoicing; and when those who bore the ark of the Lord had gone six paces, he sacrificed an ox and a fatling. And David danced before the Lord with all his might; and David was belted with a linen ephod. So David and all the house of Israel bought up the ark of the Lord with shouting and with the sound

---

[16] Chapter 23.

of the horn."[17] The idea of physically celebrating during the procession at Mass is largely unknown in the English speaking West, but if David danced with reckless abandon only because the Ark of the Covenant had entered his household, how much greater should we feel the compulsion to dance as the person who comes *in Persona Christi* proceeds to the Sanctuary of God?

While dancing should not be incorporated in Western cultures, where "dancing is tied with love, with diversion, with profaneness, with unbridling of the senses [, and] such dancing, in general, is not pure,"[18] the choice in liturgical music (antiphon or chant) during the procession should at minimum be a song that has the full potential to lift up the whole person (mind, body, and soul) to overwhelming and transformative joy.

The second grand entrance is the one that begins our Passion narratives. "Hosanna to the Son of David; blessed is he who comes in the name of the Lord; Hosanna in the highest." Each of the four Gospels attests that Jesus was met by a sizeable crowd who had given Him a king's greeting and blessing. *Luke* is the only one that departs from recording that this crowd said "Hosanna" (which means Help or Save/Give Salvation I pray) as He entered Jerusalem; that is, as they were paying homage to the Messiah-King, they were simultaneously crying out to Him for help. *Psalm* 118:25-26 is the source of this high greeting, and it is still used today in the liturgy of Jewish Seder (Passover) ritual. "In the highest," refers to the Most High - Help, I pray in the name of YHWH. *Mark's* "Blessed is he who comes in the name of the Lord! Blessed is the Kingdom of our father David that is to come!" is similar to a passage found in the Didache.[19] We should recall that not days after the Lord was so warmly received, many of these

---

[17] 2 Samuel 6:12-15.
[18] *The Religious Dance, an Expression of Spiritual Joy.* Notitiae. 11 (1975) 202-205.
[19] Cf. 10:6.

same people had chosen Barabbas over Jesus and was calling for Him to be killed by the state.

In all other Catholic Churches where I have prayed the Mass while the Priest, Deacon, and ministers are in procession, the People of God are also facing the Sanctuary where the Priest and Deacon are destined to reach (i.e., Mount Calvary), which causes them to have their back turned towards the Priest during this subject of the Divine Symphony. Such is not the case at Saint Mary's in Warren, Ohio, where when 'the Entrance' begins, the People of the Church turn to face the Priest, who acknowledges them as he makes his way to the Sanctuary. As he passes, they turn their bodies to follow him. There is no applause, no dancing, but reverence to he who has come in the name of the Lord. If you have ever been to a wedding, you will notice something very nuptial about this tradition of how the assembly receives their Priest and his retinue of ministers by standing, waiting, anticipating, and follow their coming. Even more nuptial like is what I witnessed at St. Alphonsus "Rock" Liguori Church in Saint Louis, Missouri, where the Priest and his helpers rhythmically sway on their procession to the altar; being led by a woman dressed in traditional African garb and carrying a pot of incense.

Unique as these entrances may be in Latin Church, they are consistent with the *General Instruction of the Roman Missal*, which states that the purpose of 'the Entrance' is to serve as an opening of the celebration and to "foster the unity of those who have been gathered, introduce their thoughts to the mystery of the liturgical time or festivity, and accompany the procession of the Priest and ministers."[20]

With its colors, grand vestments, odors, and dignity, the older Latin rites, such as the Dominican's Missa Cantata and the Tridentine Mass, also stirs the imagination into the mystery of

---

[20] Cf. *GIRM*, III, 47.

how God, who is beyond space and time, is seeing our ministers solemnly process to the sanctuary at the same time He is seeing His Priests and ministers throughout the ages make that same journey, as He saw His own Beloved Son process to Calvary to make one last sacrifice for all of His People. As for why the character of the entrance processional ought to be solemn, Robert Cardinal Sarah wrote:

> At the beginning of our Eucharist celebrations, how is it possible to eliminate Christ carrying His Cross and walking painfully under the weight of our sins toward the place of sacrifice? There are so many Priests who enter triumphantly and walk up toward the altar, greeting people left and right, so as to appear sympathetic. Just look at the sad spectacle of some Eucharist celebrations. . . . Why so much frivolousness and worldliness at the moment of the Holy Sacrifice? Why so much profanation and superficiality, given the extraordinary priestly grace that renders us able to make the Body and Blood of Christ substantially present by the invocation of the Spirit? Why do Prayers that concern the sacred prayers in a wash of petty, human fervor? Are Christ's words insufficient, making it necessary to multiply merely human words? In such a unique and essential sacrifice, is there any need for such a display of imagination and subjective creativity? "In praying do not heap up empty phrases as the Gentiles do; for they think that they will be heard for their many words," Jesus warns us.[21] Many fervent Christians who are moved by the Passion and death of Christ on the Cross no longer have the strength to weep or to utter a cry of pain to the Priests and Bishops who make their appearance as entertainers and set themselves up as the main protagonist of the Eucharist. These believers tell us nevertheless: "We do not want to gather with men around a man! We want to see Jesus! Show Him to us in the silence and humility of your prayer!"[22]

---

[21] Mt. 6.7.
[22] *The Power of Silence*, 237.

Now, how stark is the contrast between these two types of processions in the First Movement of the Divine Symphony? Indeed, a bright line has been drawn to distinguish between a triumphant procession towards the glory of Christ's Resurrection after His crucifixion at Calvary, versus a solemn procession on the way of tears and blood to Christ's crucifixion at Calvary.

As our Lord Jesus told His disciples, His entrance into Jerusalem would be just the beginning of the journey. "From that time Jesus began to show His disciples that He must go to Jerusalem and suffer many things from the elders and chief priests and scribes, and be killed, and on the third day be raised."[23] We see the Priest entering the assembly, and we see him processing, but we haven't asked, 'to where is he headed?' More than just a mere entrance, this is also a procession; a procession to Calvary. The moments we spent before 'the Entrance' in prayerful solitude we also shared with the Priest in his figurative Mount of Olives. "Rise and pray that you may not enter into temptation,"[24] and it was with this command that the Priest enters the assembly and follows Jesus to Calvary where the Lord will be sacrificed.

The idea of processing to the Calvary is not just a theoretical or symbolic idea. Rather, the reality of the matter is expressed in the orientation and purpose of the Church building itself. Taking rise from Jewish religious system, the New Covenant House of God incorporates both the Temple and the synagogue (in purpose and in form). In the Old Covenant the essential liturgy performed in the most sacred space of the Temple, the Holy of Holies, was the rite of atonement. It was in that space that the High Priest, removed and separated from the People by a veil, interceded for them by offering the sacrificial lamb to the Most High God for the atonement of their sins. Although the synagogues

---

[23] Mt. 16:21.
[24] Lk. 22:46.

were distinct physical structures, they persisted in unity with the Temple through its orientation and purpose, which is to assemble God's People at the foot of Mount Sinai to hear God speak through Moses. Even though the "seat of Moses" is turned toward the People, the Rabbi and all those gathered are always turned towards the Holy Temple, which is represented in the synagogue by the shrine of the Torah. Like a house of the Torah, this shrine contains a type of Ark of the Covenant, which for the Jewish People, is a kind of 'Real Presence' of God. Protected by a curtain and furnished with a menorah, which burns seven candlesticks, the shrine also contains the scrolls of the Torah, the Living Word of God.

While there are many similarities in orientation, purpose, and structure between the Temple and the synagogue, in the Church, the transformative difference between the former two with the latter is the reality and the consequences of Christ being Risen. "And the curtain of the temple was torn in two, from top to bottom."[25] That is, God becoming man, so that man might be like God, permanently resolved the gulf between them, and the veil which had separated God from His People was no more. Today, the memorial sacrifice, the People's remedy of their sin, still offered by the Priesthood alone, invites the People to participate in their silence, prayer, song, offering, and witness. In this way, the Temple has come into the synagogue, but no longer are the women discriminated against and put away to the tribunes or galleries. Today, our focal point is no longer the shrine of the Torah, but the Crucifix, the Word that became flesh. To this, Joseph Ratzinger wrote:

> The fact that we find Christ in the symbol of the rising sun is the indication of a Christology defined eschatologically. Praying toward the

---

[25] Mk. 15:38.

east means going to meet the coming Christ. The liturgy, turned toward the east effects entry, so to speak, into the procession of history towards the future, the New Heaven and the New Earth, which we encounter in Christ. It is a prayer of hope, the prayer of the pilgrim as he walks in the direction shown us by the life, Passion, and Resurrection of Christ. Thus, very early on, in parts of Christendom, the eastward direction for prayer was given added emphasis by a reference to the Cross . . . The sign of the Son of Man, of the Pierced One, is the Cross, which has now become the sign of victory of the Risen One. Thus, the symbolism of the Cross merges with that of the east. Both are an expression of one and the same faith, in which the remembrance of the Pasch of Jesus makes it present and gives dynamism to the hope that goes out to meet the One who is to come.[26]

Taking up the idea of procession towards the east being a new beginning, the Priest enters the Sanctuary through a figurative birth-canal formed by the People of God, because it was from them from whence he came, and after the Mass has ended he shall return to them. For, he cannot remain in the Sanctuary after the memorial sacrifice has concluded, no more than a High Priest could remain in the Holy of Holies after he had made an atonement for the People of God. On the contrary, the Priest is truly of the People, and his ministry is always towards, in union, and for their salvation. In this way, the Priest persists as a type-of-Christ who was born of the flesh into a faithful Jewish family and was raised according to their laws and traditions; and who, at the fullness of time, preached a Gospel first to them, which would later reach the Gentiles. This Christ Jesus, who was born into that community, ascended into Heaven and will return again to His People, just as the Priest figuratively returns.

---

[26] Ratzinger, Joseph. *The Spirit of the Liturgy*. Ignatius Press. San Francisco. 2000.69-70.

For their part, the non-ordained royal priesthood does not physically enter into the same sacred space as the Priest, but, instead, are spiritually present with him. In a figurative imitation of Christ, as the Priest comes from and lives among the People, at the appointed time he then passes through them and gatherers up their hearts, their sacrifices, their cares, their anxieties, their fears, their intentions, and all of their hopes, and takes them with him to the Calvary to offer them up to God.

Indeed, the Priest has heard and gathered all our prayers, and as the living bond that unites Christ with His People he enters the sacred space and demonstrates that sign of unity by kissing the altar, which symbolically represents Christ Jesus, "the cornerstone"[27] of the Church. This kiss also venerates the martyrs (whose relics rests within the altar) and acknowledges their sacrifices, and when performed by the Deacon this kiss functions as an extension of peace to the faithful gathered.

When the Entrance Chant has concluded, the Priest and the People of God, standing together, sign themselves with 'the Sign of the Cross', while the Priest, facing the People (if not ad orientem), says, **"In the name of the Father, and of the Son, and of the Holy Spirit."** It is by means of this Greeting that the Priest signifies the Presence of the Lord to the assembled community, and they confess their belief in that reality.

One comment should be inserted at this juncture of the exordium to the theology of the Mass about the *versus Populum* (toward the People) orientation of the Priest in the liturgy of the Novus Ordo Rite, versus all other ancient liturgies and People at prayer. It is peculiar, to the say the least, that a sacrifice would not be offered, nor a people in prayer would not face their bodies and their sacrificial offerings towards the geographic direction of God's revelation to them, which for Christians is Mount Calvary;

---

[27] Cf. Eph. 2:20.

for Jews is the Temple Mount, and for Muslims is Kaaba (the sacred house bayt al-haram) at Mecca.

As noted by Louis Bouyer[28] and Joseph Ratzinger,[29] it was from a misunderstanding of why the Priest faced the People at Saint Peter's Basilica in Rome why the liturgical renewals after the Second Vatican Council (which said nothing about "versus Populum") brought this innovative idea of an 'enclosed/but God is everywhere' Protestant-style worship, which was later normalized in the Catholic Church. On the contrary, the Priest faced the People at Saint Peter's, not to create a circle of community prayer or to convert the memorial sacrifice into a communal meal, but, rather, simply because the altar/sanctuary of the Church had been constructed in the geographical West. Therefore, for the Priest to pray, as ancients have, towards the place of God's revelation, he had to face the People, but "even when the orientation of the Church enabled the celebrant to pray, turned toward the People, when at the altar, we must not forget that it was not the Priest alone who, then, turned East: it was the whole congregation, together with him."[30]

Cardinal Sarah drew from Xavier Accart's *Comprendre et Vivre la Liturgie* [Understanding and Living the Liturgy] to give a note of the testimony to the history the Churches and the People oriented to the East:[31]

> "When we stand to pray, we turn toward the east," Saint Augustine explains, echoing a tradition that goes back, according to Saint Basil to the Apostles themselves. Since the Churches were designed for the prayer of the first Christian communities, the *Apostolic Constitutions* recommended in the fourth century that they be "oriented." And when

---

[28] Bouyer, Louis. *Liturgy and Architecture.* Notre Dame Press. Notre Dame, Indiana. 1967. 53-54.
[29] *The Spirit of the Liturgy*, 78-79.
[30] *Liturgy and Architecture,* 55-56.
[31] *The Power of Silence*, 132- 133.

the altar is in the West, as in Saint Peter's Basilica in Rome, the celebrant must turn toward the rising of the sun and thus be facing the People. The concern of the Church Fathers, therefore, was not so much to celebrate with one's back or face to the People . . . but rather to face East.

Then he adds:

This bodily orientation of prayer, however, is only the sign of an interior "orientation." Origen emphasizes – does he not? – that such a choice "symbolizes the soul that looks toward the rising of the true light" when he writes in the *Gospel Parables*: "From the east the favor granted by God comes to you; for from there is the man, 'the Orient is his name',[32] who has been established 'mediator between God and man'.[33] This is for you, therefore, an invitation to 'look toward the east'[34] always whence rises for you the 'Sun of righteousness,' when the light is born for you; so that you might never 'walk in the darkness' and 'the last day' may not overtake you in darkness.[35]

Turning back to the Novus Ordo Rite, what is true and beautiful about the *versus Populum* orientation is that now the altar of sacrifice serves as the focal point of all prayers and confessions of the People, just as the shrine of the Torah in the synagogue serves as their focal point of Jewish People's attention and action. In this way, while the Priest, the People, and the offerings, may not face geographically Eastward, all our 'lifted up' hearts and our hopes are truly turned towards the seat of God's revelation on the altar. Such an orientation is symbolized all the greater when the Crucifix is placed on top or hanging directly above the

---

[32] Zac 6:12 (Douay-Rheims).
[33] 1 Tim. 2:5.
[34] Bar. 4:36.
[35] Cf. Jn. 12:35, 48.

altar, so that the People will never forget the enteral sacrifice - the perfect sign of God's love; the love that is His very nature and the motive behind why He draws us into communion with Him through the *Ite, Missa est.*

It is true that none-routine events almost always have a distinguishing moment of origin that indicates to everyone involved that there has been a transformative shift in form. For example, daytime usually begins with a sunrise; courtships often begin with a first kiss; basketball games always begin with a tipoff. Therefore, it is fitting for the holiest event to unceasingly take place on Earth, to begin with a holy sign particular of the name under which the People of God have Baptized and gathered to pray and commune. Therefore, at the words, **"In the name of the Father, and of the Son, and of the Holy Spirit,"** the Priest initiates our transition in the Divine Symphony from exposition to development, which is purposed to expand upon the work of the former, but also serve as the body of the whole sonata.

As our initiation into the Mystical Body of Christ began with 'the Sign of the Cross' at the rite of Baptism, so too does the memorial sacrifice begin with a Baptismal renewal of our first confession of faith. For Joseph Ratzinger, "in the Sign of the Cross, together with the invocation of the Trinity, the whole essence of Christianity is summed up; it displays what is distinctively Christian."[36] That is, as a sign, it points to all that which essentially belongs to the summation of salvation history. Whether 'the Sign of the Cross is used in public or in Mass, it is our faithful confession that we believe in, exist by, and hope for the Holy Trinity. It is in, for, and by this love of the Triune God we are sealed.[37]

---

[36] *The Spirit of the Liturgy,* 177-184.
[37] Cf. Rev. 7:2-4, 14:1, 22:4; 2 Cor. 1:22; Eph. 1:13, 4:30; Eze. 9:4.

For these reasons, 'the Sign of the Cross' enjoys an intentional liberality in the liturgies of both the Eastern and the Western rites. By intentional I mean to say that this sign should never be offered flippantly or with any hint of kittenishness. As can be witnessed on at given Sunday Mass, it has most certainly become the custom of some in the Western rites to lazily make the most half-hearted 'Sign of the Cross' as they kneel before the altar prior to taking their seat; and similarly, in the Eastern rites after they enter the Church building. On the contrary, all confessions, most especially those belonging to the sacraments and their renewals, ought to be taken seriously and never be used as a time to be cute or glib. If you are going to make 'the Sign of the Cross' at any time, do it with a heart of conviction, in remembrance of your promise and in honor of the Names of which you speak; the Names that are above any other names on Earth or in Heaven.

Then, as an outward sign of intercession, the Priest extends his hands, greets the People, saying, **"The grace of our Lord Jesus Christ, and the love of God, and the communion of the Holy Spirit be with you all."**[38] By this blessing and the Royal Priesthood's response blessing upon their Priest, **"And with your spirit,"** the mystery of the Church gathered together is made manifest."[39] That is, what is a mystery of how the People of God, throughout salvation history and space and time, have now been gathered into the Body of Christ through the Holy Spirit, is now, here at the Mass, readily perceivable through the senses. At this moment, the gathered community beholds the immediate Presence of God with His People, through His grace, love, and indwelling. The shorter optional blessing, **"The Lord be with you,"** will be repeated five times during the four movements of the Divine Symphony; thereby, signally each time a new liturgical escalation in

---

[38] Cf. 2 Cor. 13:14.
[39] *GIRM*, III, 50.

the principal matter of the Sacrifice of the Mass, which is to make Christ Jesus present to His People.

The sacred Scriptures and the Sacrifice of the Mass are deeply rooted in each other, and here, out of the Pauline tradition of opening greetings, we witness one example (with a few exceptions) of their intertwined roots. The immediate distinction from the Apostle is that the Priest is not called to introduce himself to the Church, as Saint Paul would have typically announced himself to be an apostle or slave of Jesus Christ in the opening of each of his letters. The Catholic Priest does not do that at the opening of the memorial sacrifice because who the Priest is of no regard sacramentally. Therefore, to introduce himself here could risk making the Mass an effort at individualism; as if he is not acting *in Persona Christi* or as if the sacrament is from work of the doer (*ex opere operantis*), rather than from work of the work (*ex opere operato*). To the contrary, what is very similar to the Pauline tradition is the Priest's greeting of opening blessings and where he extends to the People of God the words 'grace and peace to you from God our Father and the Lord Jesus Christ.'[40]

"And with your spirit" is the first of many liturgical 'call and responses' or 'dialogue of persons' or 'antiphonals', and it is one of the most visible signs that the People of God are devoid of any singularity or division; for, they are truly brothers and sisters of one another.[41] This one liturgical voice of the communion saints and sinners being made saints is the one voice that connects all of them throughout salvation history. Together we are the People of Moses who charged at Mount Sinai, after the hearing the Lord's commands, saying, "Everything the Lord has said, we will do." We are the same People who stood as Ezra read from the

---

[40] Cf. 1 Cor. 1:3; 2 Cor. 1:2; Gal 1:3; Eph. 1:2, Phil. 1:2; Col. 1:2; 1 Thess. 1:1, 2 Thess. 1:2; 1 Tim. 1:2; 2 Tim. 1:2.
[41] Cf. *GIRM*, III, 95.

book of the law from daybreak until midday from "a wooden plat-form that had been made for the occasion,"[42] and said, "Amen, amen!" at its hearing before we knelt and "bowed before the Lord,"[43] with our faces to the ground. We join in with the heav-enly hosts and angels at Mass in their joyful of praise, singing, "Glory to the God in the highest and Earth peace to those on whom his favor rests."[44] We are the ones whom John saw in his vision: "Then I heard every creature in Heaven and on Earth and under the earth and in the sea, everything in the universe, cry out: "To the one who sits on the throne and to the Lamb be bless-ing and honor, glory and might, forever and ever."[45] In this way, the call and responses that occur during the memorial sacrifice are singular to our universe in all that they contain and effect throughout space and time.

In the classical era, periodic phrasing was a type of call and response that compositions often employed. They consisted of an antecedent as a question phrase, which was immediately fol-lowed by a consequent phrase. Beautifully balanced in length, these phrases sound like a question and answer, or a call and re-sponse being played on musical instruments. The first subject of Mozart Wolfgang Amadeus' Symphony no. 40 contains a great example of the 'call and response' in classical symphony music. Along with his famed symphonies, the Catholic Austrian Mozart (1756 – 1791) also composed more than sixty pieces of sacred music; the majority of which were written between 1773 and 1781 while he was employed by the Prince-Archbishop of Salz-burg as the court musician.

To offer a more precise delineation in what Catholics are par-ticipating in during these 'periodic phrasings', it may be helpful to

---

[42] Neh. 8:4.
[43] Neh. 8:6.
[44] Lk. 2:14.
[45] Rev. 5:13.

look at what Black American Protestants, most famous for their 'call and response' tradition, are doing through their form of homiletics that has, at its center, a keynote (theme/phrase) that the preacher will continually repeat throughout his or her sermon.

Once, when I was still a Protestant, I attended a church service at which the guest preacher used the narratives about Jesus clearing out the Temple area, to drive home his oft-repeated theme, which was "Jesus ain't no punk." It was amazing how much the congregation loved that message! Of course, they all stood up and insisted, rather dared, the preacher to continue on. "Preach that word," they yelled at him. "I don't think y'all hear me," he taunted them back. I remember noticing that the assembly seemed to be exhilarated as they participated in this back and forth dialogue with the preacher. "Tell the person next to you that, Jesus wasn't no punk," he insisted; drawing his hearers in deeper; vesting them into his personal liturgy. It was like a sleeping giant had just been awoken after a five-hundred-year rest or a caveman discovering fire for the first time. For my part, I couldn't stop laughing as I shook my head in complete agreement. It was true, I mused to myself, 'Jesus was truly God and truly man, which means that He was also fully Divine and fully masculine, without any God or gender confusion.

In all non-Catholic religions that profess the divinity of Jesus Christ, the 'call and response' action within the liturgy merely serves as a dialogue between the preacher and the assembly. He or she is talking to them, and they are responding back to the preacher or to each other; usually not with the words of Christ and never the words of the universal People of God. For this reason, Protestantism never rises above the circle of man and into the sacred and transcendental; nor do their mouths or words participate in any form of instrumentality for God's grace.

To contrast, in the Catholic Church, the 'call and response' action is a real dialogue between Christ and His People. Truly, we are responding to the Priest who is *in Persona Christi*, and he speaks to us in that Name. That is, when the Priest opens the Mass by saying, **"The grace of our Lord Jesus Christ, and the love of God, and the communion of the Holy Spirit be with you all"** those words are potent, living, active, efficacious, and able to perform what they propose if we receive them, because it is genuinely Christ speaking them to us through the Priest who is immediately participating in the Lord's ministry to His People. Similarly, the People of God gathered together represent the Presence of Jesus Christ, and they also participate in His ministry by affirming the prayers of the Mass and by extending Christ's peace to one another.

In the history of Catholic liturgy, the Novus Ordo Mass has the largest number of call and responses between the laity and the Priest. I know for some who prefer the older Masses, this dialogue with the Priest is disconcerting. I also know that there is a learning curve in regard to this liturgy for those who don't know when or how to respond. Yet, if the Priest is *In Persona Christi* and dialogue with God is essential to our becoming like God, then I must contend that this is one thing that the Novus Ordo has gotten supremely correct.

In sacred Scripture, the very first dialogue takes place when God is about to create humanity. Up until that point in *Genesis* chapter 1, God utters His creative word, but there is no dialogue of persons, until He says, "Let us make human beings in our image, after our likeness. Let them have dominion over the fish of the sea, the birds of the air, the tame animals, all the wild animals, and all the creatures that crawl on the Earth."[46] The response to this call was the great movement of creation. Therefore, it ought

---

[46] Gn. 1:26.

to be drawn from this transition that the creation of humanity necessitated a conversation within the mutual will of the Holy Trinity that was not necessary at any other point prior to. It was this spoken dialogue about the nature, essence, and call of man that lovingly moved God to act on our behalf voluntarily.

This very first dialogue would go on to serve as a model of grace. For, at every point of salvation history, whenever God desired to act on our behalf, a necessary dialogue would first take place, which oftentimes began with a call and response. Whether that dialogue was with Abraham, Isaac, Jacob, Moses, David, Job, Jonah, Jeremiah, Mary or Jesus, God always condescended to speak to His People in their own language; in the vernacular; in a manner that they would be able to acquiesce or respond to. Even after God stepped into our lives as one of us, Mary and Joseph taught Him how to communicate in Hebrew and Aramaic, so that He could understand and be understood by those in His family and community. The arch-Angel Gabriel told Mary to name her son Yeshua (יֵשׁוּעַ, meaning 'God saves'), which was a name that His family and community could understand. When Christ Jesus began His ministry, He proclaimed and evangelized the good news in the local vernacular. He renamed Simon ben Yonah (שמעון, meaning 'heard') Kephas (כאפא, meaning 'rock'). The text of the Gospels often uses actual Aramaic words that Jesus spoke. When Jesus celebrated the last Seder Passover feast with His disciples, He didn't offer it in Greek or Latin; rather, it was in the local vernacular that He said, "This is my body, which will be given for you; do this in memory of Me".[47] Therefore, there is obviously something very important to God about speaking to His People in their own language. Moreover, it demonstrates the humility of God; how there is no learning curve necessary to encounter Him.

---

[47] Lk. 22:19.

Being that the Mass is the highest form of Christian prayer and prayer is necessary for salvation, and dialogue with God mutually benefits the Divine and human desire for the latter's salvation, the liturgy of Christ Jesus' own Church must be able and willing to meet all People where they are and afford them with the opportunity to dialogue with God regardless of their circumstances and limitations.

Communication barriers are one such limitation that may pose some difficulty for some to overcome. In fact, it was not until Christ came with His Church that the communication barrier that God Himself established at the Tower of Babel was permanently torn down at the New Covenant Pentecost. "Come, let us go down, and there confuse their language, and they may not understand one another's speech."[48] "And they were all filled with the Holy Spirit and began to speak in other tongues, as the Spirit gave them utterance."[49] The gift of speaking tongues that the Apostles received at the birth of Church is also a sign of the diversity of liturgy that can hear God speak in their own language.

Indeed, what permanently resolved Babel was the Admirable Exchange; that is, the beautiful mystery of the Incarnation of the Divine nature taking on human nature; of God becoming man, so that man might become like God. Through the Admirable Exchange, perfected in sacrifice on the Cross, Christ Jesus permanently took up and elevated human nature into the Divine so that there would never again be a broken bridge between God and man. For, Christ Jesus Himself becomes that bridge that heals the breach and barrier that separates the otherness of these two natures.

In this regard, the curse of Babel must be considered along with the same lines as the curse brought upon Adam and Eve for

---

[48] Gn. 11:7.
[49] Acts 2:4.

their disobedience, in the sense that at the very moment God imposes a wound in a community or a person, He simultaneously prepares a way for that wound to be healed. If such a simultaneous path is not prepared, then He isn't God; rather, He is merely a cruel sadist. More than that, the Sacrament of the Mass itself, being the fullest expression on Earth of God's plan for salvation, healing, and communion between the Divine and human, it must demonstrate that He has healed our inability to communicate; otherwise, the liturgy doesn't very reflect well on God.

It is true. When Christ Jesus took up the human nature into the Divine, He did not just take up some parts or aspects of it. Instead, He took up all of what makes us human; that is, our soul, our emotions, our intellect, our memories, our capacities of self, and, yes, our language. In taking up the human language into the Divine, God finally gave His creatures the capacity to speak the truth. He gave man and woman the ability to express the reality of the Divine thing in our own language that had now become His language. God healed the curse of Babel through the Mass by demonstrating that the highest form of communication (communion) is not between men alone. Rather, we were created for communion in and through God for His glory.

Through the incarnation, Jesus, the Divine Logos, marries the Divine language with our human language by speaking only what His Eternal Father gave Him to speak. Through this, His earthly ministry became an exchange of dialogue (from the Gk. dialogos; meaning through speak) with those who would hear Him. He became the par excellence example of the new human capacity to use our elevated language to be an ongoing source of healing for Babel. In commissioning us to teach the world all that He taught us,[50] He was inspiring us to build the Church as the new Tower of Babel in a sense. That is, a place where our healed

---

[50] Cf. Mt. 28:20.

languages provoke us not to "build ourselves a city, and a tower with its top in the Heavens,"[51] but, rather, a city of God and a Church that points to Calvary.

When Jesus took up human language and gave to it the capacity to express the truth of the Divine, He didn't just take up His native earthly language. He didn't just take up Hebrew or Aramaic. He didn't just take up Greek, Latin, and Farsi. He didn't just take up languages not commonly spoken at the time, such as Spanish and English. No, He took up all human languages spoken throughout all of existence, so that there would always be a way for humans to call on the name of Yeshua in any language and be heard.

In this way, the Novus Ordo Mass is a wonderful example of the Admirable Exchange and the healing of Babel. The language used at the Mass is always the common language of the People of God there gathered and is also a language that God has healed to speak of Him in truth and love. It is also the very same language that Christ Jesus elevated to the Divine so that families, communities, and nations could speak with each other in words that unite and bless. Therefore, the Novus Ordo Mass teaches us how to speak to each other in the vernacular outside of the Mass in a manner which gives glory to God.

It also true that the liturgical rites such as the Tridentine, Byzantine, Antiochian, Melkite, Ruthian, and etc., that celebrate in only one language, also heal the curse of Babel by uniting the faithful in one tongue. The fact that there are so many of these singular language liturgies, but only 'one' Sacrifice of the Mass is a Divinely beautify thing.

---

[51] Gen. 11:4.

THE PENITENTIAL RITE TO THE COLLECT

The Priest calls those who are assembled to ready themselves to offer a public confession of their sins, by saying, **"Brothers and sisters, let us acknowledge our sins, and so prepare ourselves to celebrate the sacred mysteries."** This moment in the Mass should harken us all back to the eviction day of Adam and Eve from the Garden of Eden, and how they were without word or rebuttal as God pronounced His sentence. We too are without word before we make our public confession, because we are being called to reflect momentarily in silence on those sins that separates us from God who we are about to pray to receive most audaciously.

In the book of *Genesis*, "the LORD said: My spirit shall not remain in human beings forever, because they are only flesh. Their days shall comprise one hundred and twenty years."[52] Yet, in the New Covenant, the Holy Spirit dwells within the Baptized, and Christ Jesus' Eucharistic promise is that our days will be eternal. It is worthy to reflect upon, that if Eve's eating from the Tree of Life in a disordered and unworthy manner caused punishment and sin to enter the world, what wrath of God is being reaped on those who eat the Holy Eucharist unworthily?

This Divine law stretches all the way back into the Old Covenant, where it was warned, "If however, someone in a state of uncleanness eats the meat of a communion sacrifice belonging to the Lord, that person shall be cut off from the People."[53] To be 'cut off' from the Jewish People of God is to be dead to them. In union with this law the Apostle wrote to the Church of Corinth:

> "Therefore, whoever eats the bread or drinks the cup of the Lord unworthily will have to answer for the body and blood of the Lord. A person should examine himself, and so eat the bread and drink the cup.

---

[52] Gen. 6:3.
[53] Lev. 7:20.

For anyone who eats and drinks without discerning the body, eats and drinks judgment on himself. That is why many among you are ill and infirm, and a considerable number are dying. If we discerned ourselves, we would not be under judgment; but since we are judged by [the] Lord, we are being disciplined so that we may not be condemned along with the world."[54]

So that we might prepare ourselves to celebrate the sacred mysteries and to receive the Holy Eucharist worthily, we must first be confident that we are without grave attachment to sin by receiving absolution through the Sacrament of Penance and Reconciliation, and, second to pray for forgiveness from any other types of sins that might make us less than fully open to the graces of the Divine Symphony. In the performance of the latter is why the Priest calls upon the whole community to take part in the Penitential Act through an act of public confession of sins by way of the 'Confiteor' or through one of the other prescribed options.

Just as Simon Cephas made two confessions about his faith in and love of Christ Jesus,[55] so too does the liturgies of the Tridentine and Novus Ordo rites compel us to make two confessions. The first confession found here in 'the Confiteor' concerns the harm we have voluntarily inflicted upon God, neighbor, and self through our sins. The second confession will come later through the Creed, where we confess our belief in the one Baptism through which our sins were forgiven and through which we were redeemed into the Body of Christ. In the Divine Liturgy of the Byzantine Rite (also called the Divine Liturgy of Saint John Chrysostom) the laity only make the one confession found in the Creed, while the Priest and Deacon make several confessions,

---

[54] 1 Cor. 11:27-32.
[55] Cf. Mt. 16:16; Jn. 21:15-17.

with three of them echoing Simon Cephas, beginning with the words, "O Lord, I believe and confess . . ."

The placement, participants, arrangement of words, and repetition of the 'I confess' has been varied throughout history and rite. In the Eastern liturgies a type of 'Confiteor' has always been a prayer for mercy, forgiveness of sins and transgressions, said by the Celebrant alone (or with the Deacon), either before the doors are opened or at the very opening of the Mass, and does not include any appeal to the Church Triumphant or to the Church Suffering. In the Mass of Trent, the 'Confiteor' begins, "I confess to Almighty God, to blessed Mary ever Virgin, to blessed Michael the Archangel, to blessed John the Baptist, to the holy Apostles Peter and Paul, to all the Saints, and to you, brethren . . ." In that rite, the confession is said first by the Celebrant and then by the altar server, with the Priest ending his confession to "the brethren," and the altar server's ending theirs to "father."

In the Novus Ordo, 'the Confiteor' meets the East and the West by beginning with a confession to God and to the Church Suffering, "I confess to almighty God and to you, my brothers and sisters, that I have greatly sinned . . ." and then ends with an entreaty to the Church Triumphant and the Church Suffering for prayers, "therefore I ask blessed Mary ever-Virgin, all the Angels, and Saints, and you, my brothers and sisters, to pray for me to the Lord our God." In this arrangement, the 'Confiteor' affirms that sin is first an action that damages our relationship with God, with the Church (the Body of Christ), and with our neighbors. Moreover, it calls us to audaciously ask from those whom we have harmed for their mercy and prayers; thereby, witnessing to the wisdom of God who created People to help People get to Heaven. To honestly know that we have sinned is to be genuinely remorseful enough to publicly confess it in word "through my fault, through my fault, through my most grievous fault" (mea culpa, mea culpa, mea maxima culpa) and in sign by beating our breast in excoriation of our failings in all areas that we may have fallen into sinful thoughts, words, actions (what I have done), and inaction (what I have failed to do). For this, the Baptized then asks the *Theotokos* – the ever-Virgin Mother of God, the Church Triumphant - those who have had victory through this confession In Christ, and the Church Suffering who are with them on this pilgrimage to pray on their behalf to their only source of help - our Savior and Redeemer.

It has been the tradition in some Catholic Churches, prior to 'the Entrance' to call the People to recite a prayer of one our saints that intends to prepare us for the memorial sacrifice. While these practices are not necessarily harmful or undermining, they are completely unnecessary, because they lack the protection and grace afforded to 'the Confiteor' and the Priest's own prayers of intercession

As a form of public confession, 'the Confiteor' unites the Church as a community of repentant sinners who have come to the throne of God to beg for His mercy, healing, and forgiveness. They come here not hoping for this remedy of their chronic condition, but, rather in knowing that the liturgy is leading and guiding them to the balm of Gilead that they will find in the Holy Eucharist.

After this first liturgical confession, the Priest then concludes the Penitential Rite by granting a sacramental absolution to all those who have publicly confessed; saying, **"May almighty God have mercy on us, forgive us our sins, and bring us to everlasting life."** This sacramental absolution, however, lacks the efficacy of the Sacrament of Penance and Reconciliation.

One way to consider the distinction between sacramental absolution at Mass and the Sacrament of Penance and Reconciliation is by viewing it similar to when the blessing and sprinkling of water takes place in the Penitential Rite during Easter Season and at other times. There, the sprinkling by the Priest on the

People publicly assembled does not actually grant the Sacrament of Baptism. Likewise, neither does public confession during the Penitential Rite grant full absolution of grave sins that only the Sacrament of Penance and Reconciliation effects.

Another way to better understand why this sacramental absolution out of the Penitential Rite lacks the efficacy of the absolution out of the Sacrament of Penance is by examining the five elements of offering and petition in the 'Our Father' prayer that Christ Jesus taught His disciples.[56] The first element is offering reverence to Fatherhood of God and to the Holiness of His name ("Our Father in Heaven, Holy is your name"). The second element is offering to cooperate with the work of God ("Thy Kingdom come; Thy will be done . . ."). The third element is petitioning God for the spiritual and material sustenance we need to cooperate with His work ("Give us this day, our daily bread . . ."). The fourth element is petitioning God to forgive us of any sins that will impede us from loving Him, our neighbor, and self as we ought, and, thereby, might cause us to stumble in cooperating with God ("and forgive us of our sin as we forgive those who have sinned against us . . ."). The final element is petitioning God for the graces and help that will always allow us to avoid evil and the tests of Job so that we might always be free to pursue His work alone ("and lead us not into temptation, but deliver us from evil").

Being that the Mass is the highest form of Christian prayer and that it contains the fulfillment of the Passover sacrifice, four of the five elements of the 'Our Father' prayer take on their highest form within the liturgy of the Mass and become offerings and petitions par excellence. That is, there is no higher way to offer reverence to God than through the liturgy of the Mass; there is no higher way to offer to cooperate with God than through the prayers and Sacrifice of the Mass; there is no higher petitioning

---

[56] Cf. Mt. 6:9-13; Lk. 11:1-4.

of God for material and spiritual sustenance, because in the Mass we truly receive the daily and eternal Bread of Life; and there is no higher way to petition God for help to persevere in His work than through the Mass, which itself is the great sacramental *misso* (sending).

Yet, the fourth element of the 'Our Father'; the petitioning of God to forgive us of any sins that will impede us from loving Him, our neighbor, and self as we ought, is the only element that does not find its highest form in the liturgy of the Mass. On the contrary, the form, par excellence, of the highest way that we could ever petition God for forgiveness and healing from the harm that sin causes the soul and body is through the through the Sacrament of Penance and Reconciliation.

One of the oldest prayers in the Divine Symphony is 'the Kyrie Eleison.' Its first documented use in liturgy comes from the Eighth Book, Chapter Seven, of *Apostolic Constitutions*, which can be dated circa 375/380 AD and attributed to Syria or Antioch.[57] Like the *Didache*, the *Didascalia Apostolorum*, and others, the *Apostolic Constitutions* belongs to a genre of Catholic-oriented literature that attempted to offer an authoritative (i.e., Apostolic) guide over Christian life, liturgy, and Church governance. William A. Jurgens called the *Apostolic Constitutions* a work of "forgery of the grosser and more impious sort," because it used the name of Clement, Bishop, and Citizen of Rome, not as "mere a congenial literary device," but, instead, as an attempt deceive.[58]

Despite the spurious origins of the *Apostolic Constitutions*, its witness to 'the Kyrie Eleison' as an early liturgical response to prayers, points to the fact that the liturgy of the Catholic Mass, regardless of the rite, has always consisted of a series of holy

---

[57] Bradshaw, Paul F. (2002). The Search for the Origins of Christian Worship. Oxford University Press. 85–87.
[58] Jurgens, William A. *The Faith of the Early Fathers*. Volume II. The Liturgical Press, Collegeville, Minnesota. 1979. 127.

prayers and contrite confessions. To be certain, nothing is more troubling and harmful than a Catholic who believes that the Mass is merely a cacophony of disjointed 'things we do,' 'prayers we say,' 'prayers the Priest says,' 'times we stand,' and 'times we kneel.' For, if that is all the Mass is, then God deserves much better than something not inspired by Him.

To the contrary, the Mass is the highest form of Christian prayer, and prayer is completely empty if it does not cry out for mercy. Confession is a barren ocean if it does not cry out for mercy. Therefore, it is right that 'the Kyrie Eleison' should follow the 'Confiteor.' In this spirit and with the People of God gathered, we cry out in chant or song 'Kyrie Eleison' at least twice to each acclamation. Yet, this petition can never be repeated enough. Should the choir or cantor one day refuse to be moved from chanting the 'Kyrie Eleison' for an hour, it would be an hour not wasted. In the Ambrosian Rite, the opening procession stops in the middle of the nave to sing 'the Kyrie Eleison' twelve times, before continuing on to Calvary. In the Divine Liturgy of the Byzantine Rite, this cry for God's mercy is asked for at least four dozen times, and for them, that is still not enough.

In confessing 'the Confiteor', we offer to God that we are no better than His beloved David who said to Nathan, "I have sinned against the Lord," and in praying the 'Kyrie Eleison' we cry out like David who, for six days, fasted and wept, hoping against hope that God would show him mercy. On the seventh day, David rose up and proclaimed the sovereignty of God who shows His love, grace, and mercy upon His children according to His will. David was penitent in regard to his adultery with Bathsheba, and God kept His word by striking down the fruit of their sin, but He did not forsake David. Rather, according to His will, He blessed him with a son named Solomon.[59] Like David, we too are humbled by

---

[59] Cf. 2 Sam. 12.

the sovereignty of God and hope against hope that He smiles upon our life.

The last two parts of the Divine sonata are 'the Gloria in Excelsis Deo' and 'the Collect,' and their purpose is to serve as a recapitulation. In a symphony orchestra, the recapitulation is the most important section of the sonata because it closes this part of the symphony by presenting its central argument or major elements by literally repeating/restating or by reinterpreting/shuffling them. In this same way, the 'Gloria in Excelsis Deo' and 'the Collect' reiterate and close all that the People have prayed and confessed in 'the Greeting' and 'the Penitential Act.'

As David moved from confession to begging for mercy to joyful praise, so too do we move from the 'Confiteor' and the 'Kyrie Eleison' to 'the Gloria in Excelsis Deo', except during the seasons and Lent and Advent and for other solemnities and feasts, when the Church calls our soul to remain contrite and solemn.

"Glory to God in the highest, and on Earth peace to People of good will.[60] We praise you,[61] we bless you,[62] we worship you (Lat. adorámus te),[63] we glorify you,[64] we give you thanks for your great glory,[65] Lord God, heavenly King,[66] O God, almighty Father.[67] Lord Jesus Christ, Only Begotten

---

[60] Lk. 2:14.

[61] Cf. 1 Ch. 29:13; Ps. 79:13.

[62] Cf. Jdg. 5:2, 9; 1 Ch. 29:20; Neh. 9:5, Ps. 16:7, 26:12, 34:1, 103:1, 2, 20, 21, 104:35, 115:18, 134:1, 135:19, 20.

[63] Cf. Exo. 12:31; 1 Sam. 15:25, 30; 1 Ch. 16:29; Ps. 2:11, 29:2, 96:9; Isa. 27:13; Jer. 7:2; Mt. 4:10; Lk. 4:8.

[64] Cf. Jn. 21:19, Rom. 15:9; 1 Cor. 6:20; 2 Cor. 9:13; 1 Pet. 2:12, 4:16.

[65] Cf. Lev. 7:12, 13, 15, 22:29; Neh. 12:46; Ps. 26:7, 42:4, 50:14, 23, 69:30, 95:3, 107:22, 116:17, Jer. 17:26, 30:19, Jon. 2:9, 2 Cor. 9:11, Col. 1:3, 4:2; 1 Thess. 1:2, 2 Thess. 1:3, 2:13; Phl 4:6; Rev. 7:12.

[66] Cf. Gen. 14:22; 2 Ch. 36:23; Ezr. 1:2; Neh. 2:4, Dan. 2:37, 4:37.

[67] Cf. Gen. 49:25, Isa. 9:6.

Son,[68] Lord God, Lamb of God,[69] Son of the Father,[70] you take away the sins of the world,[71] have mercy on us;[72] you take away the sins of the world, receive our prayer; you are seated at the right hand of the Father,[73] have mercy on us. For you alone are the Holy One,[74] you alone are the Lord,[75] you alone are the Most High,[76] Jesus Christ, with the Holy Spirit, in the glory of God the Father. Amen."

Beginning with what the multitude of heavenly hosts said in praise of God at the birth of Yeshua, "Glory to God in the highest and on Earth peace among men with whom he is pleased,"[77] 'the Gloria in Excelsis Deo' is a liturgical formula of praise to God, consisting of a collection of many verses of sacred Scripture. The oldest use of 'the Gloria' comes from the East where the Greek is still used in the Byzantine Rite during the Orthros (Matins), Sundays, and feast days. According to one tradition, the very similar Latin translation of this doxology found its way to the West by way of Saint Hilary of Poiters (c. 300 – 368), who may have learned of it during his period of exile (360). Yet, according to another tradition, Pope Saint Telesphorus (125 – 136), who is accredited with introducing the Midnight Mass of Christmas and made fasting during Lent obligatory, is the one who placed 'the

---

[68] Jn. 3:16, 18; Heb. 11:17; 1 Jn. 4:9.
[69] Jn. 1:29, 36.
[70] 2 Jn. 1:3.
[71] Cf. 1 Jn. 3:5.
[72] Mt. 9:27, 20:30, 31; Lk. 17:13.
[73] Cf. Lk. 22:69; Eph. 1:20; Col. 3:1.
[74] Cf. Mk. 1:24; Lk. 4:34.
[75] Cf. Jn. 20:28; 1 Cor. 12:3; Phil. 3:8.
[76] Note: This title of Jesus is one of the entries that does not belong to the original Greek. Jesus is never called the Most High in sacred Scripture, but He does come from the only begotten Son of the Most High. Cf. Mk. 5:7; Lk. 1:32, 35, 8:28.
[77] Lk. 2:14.

Gloria' in the Latin liturgy.[78] It wouldn't be until centuries later when Pope Saint Symmachus (November 22, 498 – July 19, 514) ordered that 'the Gloria in Excelsis Deo' to be sung at all Sunday Masses and martyrs' feast days.[79]

During a podcast that I was hosting many years ago, a woman who had converted to Catholicism from Mormonism had expressed during her interview how much she loves the 'Gloria in Excelsis Deo' "because it says everything." I couldn't quite completely understand what she meant by that at the time, because I had not yet connected the 'Gloria in Excelsis Deo' to the recapitulation of a sonata. Yet, she was absolutely correct in her sentiments that this harmonious collection of prayers and confessions which attests to the glory and Tri-unity of God, does, indeed, proclaim what is truly unique to Christianity. It most certainly does 'confess everything' for Christians, similar to how the *Shema*[80] 'confessed everything' for Jews.

Even on a deeper level, if we examine what it truly is that are we confessing in the 'Gloria in Excelsis Deo', we discover that we are confessing who God is, and in that sense when we sing 'the Gloria' we become a type of Simon Kephas who answered Jesus' question, "But who do you say that I am?" by confessing back to Him whom he believed He is, "You are the Christ, the Son of the living God."[81]

What I have learned in my life and what I have witnessed in the lives of others who have attentively grown in deeper knowledge of God, is exactly what we learned by reading about this first confession of Saint Peter. That is, when we confess to God who He is to us, He blesses us, because, again, God trips

---

[78] Coulombe, Charles A. *A History of the Popes. Vicars of Christ.* MJF Books. New York. 2003. 27.
[79] *A History of the Popes. Vicars of Christ,* 90.
[80] A prayer specifically commanded in the Torah, which consists of three Biblical passages: Dt. 6:4-9, 11:13-21; and Nm. 15:37-41.
[81] Mt. 16:16.

over Himself in trying to reveal Himself to us. God wants nothing more than for us to grow in the knowledge of His love and truth, and when we 'get it,' when we grow in that knowledge, He blesses us for that matriculation. Therefore, in praying the 'Gloria in Excelsis Deo,' the liturgy of the Mass sets us up for the first installment in an avalanche of blessings and graces to come.

When the 'Gloria in Excelsis Deo' has been concluded, the Priest, with his hands joined, says, **"Let us pray."** To which the People of God acclaim, **"Amen."** *Oremus* (Latin for 'Let us pray'), the call to pray, is only said twice in the Tridentine and Novus Ordo but is made over two dozen of times in the Byzantine Rite.

As the Priest and the People pray in silence here, following the conclusion of the Introductory rites, God's silent presence returns to the Divine Symphony to remind us that He remains with us as we transition to hearing His word proclaimed.

After this period of silence, the Priest then, taking the orans posture of outstretching his arms, offers one prayer that is traditionally "addressed to God the Father, through Christ, in the Holy Spirit, and is concluded with a Trinitarian ending, or longer ending..."[82] This 'Collect' prayer is intended to guide and direct the hearts of the People of God towards the unique characteristics of the liturgy for that day; thereby, preparing us to receive the full banquet of graces and gifts readily available to us through the sacrament of the Mass.

---

[82] *GIRM*, III, 54.

The Second Movement
of
The Divine Symphony

EXORDIUM TO THE
LITURGY OF THE WORD

Following the first movement of the Divine Symphony enters the second slower movement in the Liturgy of the Word with the purpose of feeding us with the words of God, so that we might receive The Word that became Flesh. Similar to a classical symphony, this second movement of the *Ite, Missa Est* offers a contrasting tempo, style, and presentation than we had witnessed in the former. It is also both independent and transitory to the whole piece; that is, it stands alone as a liturgical device to present the written Word of God but simultaneously is seamlessly connected as an expansion of the Introductory rites, and as a staging ground for the Liturgy of the Eucharist.

According to their own liturgical calendar and cycle of readings, every rite of the Church presents to God's People His inspired word. Yet, regardless of the expression of the memorial sacrifice, the necessary and seamless relationship between the Liturgy of the Word and the Liturgy of the Eucharist cannot be understated, because we are not talking about two things here, such as, has been the custom to refer to these parts as distinct and divergent tables. Rather, these two things are movements in one Divine Symphony; Divine sentences that depend on each other to bring out the fullness of God's offering. In his *Sacramentum Caritatis*, Pope Benedict XVI explained the necessary relationship between the Liturgy of the Word and the Liturgy of the Eucharist in this way:

> From listening to the word of God, faith is born or strengthen; in the Eucharist, the Word made flesh gives himself to us as our spiritual flood. This, "from the two tables of the word of God and the Body of Christ, the Church receives and gives to the faithful the bread of life."
> . . . Consequently, it must constantly be kept in mind that the word of God, read and proclaimed by the Church in the liturgy, leads to the Eucharist as to its own connatural end.[1]

If we are going to use the image of two tables to explain the relationship between the Liturgy of the Word and the Liturgy of the Eucharist, we should imagine them to be the two most beautiful banquet tables that had ever been crafted in Heaven, or on Earth. We should see these tables as being wholly unique from one another, but equal in allure. Yet, as different as they are in appearance, we know them to be mystically connected in every conceivable way, even to the degree that we cannot rightly eat from one without eating from the other. To separate one table from the other would cause the other not truly to *be*.

Within sacred Scripture, there are two clear examples of the four movements of the Divine Symphony. In the Old Testament, "Ezra and the priests brought the law before the assembly, which consisted of men, women, and those children old enough to understand."[2] The place where they assembled was the Water Gates, which for Christians is a symbol of the Baptismal fount inside the Church. Before Ezra read from the scroll at the wooden

---

[1] Benedict XVI. *Sacramentum Caritatis: Post-Synod Exhortation on the Eucharist as the Source and Summit of the Church's Life and Mission).* 44.
[2] Neh. 8:2.

platform, he opened it, and all the People stood. "Ezra blessed the Lord, the great God, and all the People, their hands raised high answered, "Amen, amen!"[3] Then they knelt down and bowed before the Lord with their faces to the ground. Then as Ezra read clearly from the book of the law of God, the Levites "helped the People to understand the law ... and they gave the sense so that the People understood the reading."[4] After this liturgy of the word and homily had concluded, Nehemiah, Ezra, and the Levites ordered the People to "Go, eat rich food and drink sweet drinks, and allot portions to those who had nothing prepared, for today is holy to our Lord."[5] "And then the Levites quieted all the People, saying, "Silence! Today is holy, do not be saddened." Then all the People began to eat and drink . . ."[6] While the feast that these Jews were partaking in was not the Holy Eucharist, the events of this day apparently consisted of an opening rite, a liturgy of the law of God, a feast, which would have been concluded with some type of song, blessings, and prayer. This liturgy of Ezra is fulfilled today in the liturgy of the memorial sacrifice.

In the New Testament, the clearest example of the four movements of the Divine Symphony derives from Saint Paul's *First Letter to the Corinthians*, where in chapter 11 he offers instructions on how to celebrate the Liturgy of the Eucharist and in chapter fourteen verses twenty-six through forty he gives instructions on how the Liturgy of the Word must be conducted "decently and in order."[7] Based upon this evidence, it would be far from an unreasonable supposition that these Christians, many of whom were Jews, would have prefaced and concluded

[3] Neh. 8:6.
[4] Neh. 8:7-8.
[5] Neh. 8:10.
[6] Neh. 8:11.
[7] 1 Cor. 14:40.

these two movements with an opening and closing rite of prayers and songs just as they would have for any other of their liturgical feasts.

Outside of Scripture, the earliest attestation comes from chapter sixty-seven ('Weekly Worship of the Christians') of Saint Justin Martyr's *First Apology*, written between 152 and 155 A.D., and addressed to the Emperor Aelius Adrianus Antoninus Pius Augustus Caesar, and to his son Verissimus the Philosopher, Lucius the Philosopher, the natural son of Caesar, and the adopted son of Pilus, and to the sacred Senate of Rome. The intention of the apology was to function as a 'Christianity for Dummies' instructional in hopes to dissuade the emperor from holding hostilities against the Church, resulting from lies that had been spread about Her throughout the empire.

> And on the day called Sunday, all who live in cities or in the country gather together to one place, and the memoirs of the apostles or the writings of the prophets are read, as long as time permits; then, when the reader has finished, he who presides over those gathered admonishes and challenge them to imitate these beautiful things. Then we all rise together and offer prayer for ourselves, and, as we before said, when our prayer is ended, bread and wine and water are brought, and the president in like manner offers prayers and thanksgivings, according to his ability, and the People assent, saying Amen; and there is a distribution to each, and a participation of that over which thanks have been given, and to those who are absent a portion is sent by the Deacons.[8]

Early on in my conversion process to the Catholic Church I still visited Protestant services, because the preaching typically satisfied my craving to be both spiritually motivated and entertained, but as I began to discover the Heavenly dimensions of

---

[8] St. Justin, *Apol.* 1, 67.

what was taking place at the Mass and what I was participating in, I began to refuse to set myself up to ever be disappointed again. Having truly tasted and seen what it meant to be wholly satisfied at the banquet tables of the Catholic Mass, I desired not to position myself never again to be spiritually unsatisfied.

Indeed, to be Catholic is to know the reality of simultaneously finding our great joy and our great disappointment. That is, once a person comes to understand what is truly transpiring at the Sacrifice of the Mass, they simultaneously discover that they will never find an equal or more significant experience anywhere else on Earth. How comforting and poetically gruesome is the reality that you may never find a greater love than that which you have found? If you have ever experienced an amazing movie, there is a possibility that you may experience an even a more amazing movie in the future. There will always be an even better fitting pair of jeans, or better tasting German Chocolate Cake. One Protestant Church to the next offers nothing so unique that their other denominations can't duplicate or replicate it. Not so with the Divine Symphony! There is absolutely no other place in the universe that one may experience what it alone offers. It is so wholly fulfilling that every other experience in the world outside of it is completely disappointing.

The liturgy of memorial sacrifice is so unique to the universe that there are four Holy things that only the Church can bring together when they are joined in the Divine Symphony. Of those four, only one of them is natural to the Mass; meaning that the Mass is its original setting (where it derives from). The other three are preter-natural to the Mass; meaning that these things can also be naturally found outside of the Mass. The thing that is natural to the Mass is the Sacrament of the Holy Eucharist – the Real Body, Blood, Soul, and Divinity of Christ Jesus. The Mass is the only place where the person of Christ Jesus truly becomes the Sacrament of His Body and Blood for us to consume. There is no other place in the universe where you can witness this miracle than at the Catholic Mass. The preter-natural things also participate in the Presence of God in their own way; those three things are: (1) The Priest (Christ present in His Minister); (2) The Holy Scriptures (God Present in the Speaking His Word); and (3) The Congregation (God Present in the Baptized in whom He dwells).

Paragraph 1088 of the Catechism of the Catholic Church explains the Divine convergence of the four Holy things in this way:

> "To accomplish so great a work" – the dispensation or communication of his work of salvation – "Christ is always present in his Church, especially in her liturgical celebrations. He is present in the Sacrifice of the Mass not only in the person of his minister, 'the same now offering, through the ministry of priests, who formerly offered himself on the cross,' but especially in the Eucharistic species. By his power, He is present in the sacraments so that when anybody baptizes, it is really Christ Himself who baptizes. He is present in His word since it is He Himself who speaks when the holy Scriptures are read in the Church. Lastly, He is present when the Church prays and sings, for He has promised 'where two or three are gathered together in my name there am I in the midst of them.'"[9]

This inescapable magnanimous quad Presence of God is only present at the Sacrifice of the Mass. Everywhere we turn at the Mass, there is God, and there He is in a way that is perceptible to each of our five senses. This Divine reality reminds us of our Lord's response to the Pharisees when He said, "The coming of the kingdom of God cannot be observed, and no one will announce, 'Look, here it is,' or, 'There it is.' For behold, the kingdom of God is among you."[10]

---

[9] SC 7; Mt 18:20.
[10] Lk. 17:20-21.

"Silence! Today is holy, do not be saddened."[11] We are intentionally silent and reverent as we listen to and meditate on the written Word of God being spoken because it is His Presence and we are being drawn back again into that state of solitude where God calls each us to discover the path to grow deeper in knowledge and love of Him. Just as the Israelites prepared themselves for three days to receive the Law of the Lord,[12] so too did the prayers and confessions in the Introductory Rite prepare us for this moment. The People who heard Ezra read the law of God were saddened because hearing the word convicted them, just as it convicted King Josiah to the point of tearing his clothes at the hearing of book of the Law,[13] and so too does the Holy Spirit who dwells in us convict us at the hearing of the word of God. If this is why Catholics look so solemn and distraught during the Divine Symphony, fine, but let it not be because they are bored in the darkness of ignorance of what they are experiencing.

"So He gave orders to have them sit down in groups on the green grass."[14] While standing during the Divine Symphony offers a visible demonstration of our attention to the present matter, relaxing our bodies in a sitting posture should make us no less attentive to the mysteries before us. "Our bodies should be relaxed so that our hearing and understanding are unimpeded."[15] The Greek here in *Mark* for 'in groups' is *prasia*, which means 'a bed for leeks' (onions that are planted in straight rows). This image at the miracle of the Multiplication of Loaves and Fives of an orderly crowd of People sitting in straight rows at the feet of the Lord and waiting to be fed bread and fish feels Eucharistic, because it sings of the truth that we are entirely dependent on God,

---

[11] Neh. 8:11.
[12] Cf. Exo. 19.
[13] 2 Kgs. 22:11.
[14] Mk. 6:39.
[15] *The Spirit of the Liturgy*, 196.

and are always being fed in some way when we are in His Presence.

There is grace found in sitting down and listening to the Lord. How else could the Holy Spirit use us to lead others to Jesus Christ, unless we first become sheep who follow and respond to the words of their shepherd? Throughout the salvation history, it has been the pattern that those who are called to lead, must first sit and attend to the words of God. Recall Moses spending forty years in the desert tending the flock of his father-in-law Jethro, before he spent another forty years in the same desert tending the flock of YHWH; Joshua sitting under Moses for about forty years until the prophet died and then was called by the Lord to succeed him; the Apostles walking with Jesus for three years and then for another forty days after His resurrection before He sent them out with the power to establish His Church on Earth; the many spiritual children, students, and acquaintances of the Apostles who were hearers of their spoken words and who helped to pass down the Deposit of Faith.[16] Indeed, many Christians will attest to the fact that not long after their true conversion of heart, that the Spirit of God inspired them to be patient and sit down so that they could build a relationship with the Holy Trinity through prayer, silence, study, and receiving the Sacraments.

Lastly, as the People sit in silence at particular moments during the Divine Symphony, they do not forsake their participation in the great mystery. Instead, they truly do extend themselves deeper into it by becoming children who are being fed the words of eternal life, and by becoming witnesses to the salvation history being heard through the words that were inspired by God.

---

[16] The _Catechism of the Catholic Church_ defines _the Deposit of Faith_ as: The heritage of faith contained in sacred Scripture and Tradition, handed on in the Church from the time of the Apostles, from which the Magisterium draws all that it proposes for belief as being Divinely revealed (CCC 84; cf. 1202).

One thing we must not be ignorant of is that fact that it is only at the memorial sacrifice and only during the Liturgy of the Word where the sacred Scriptures are found and heard in their most natural environment. While the Scriptures are not preternatural to the Liturgy of the Word, it was for the Liturgy of the Word that the Catholic canon was protected, preserved, and promulgated so that it might always protect and prepare the way for the coming of the Lord. When the Scriptures are read in union with the memory of the sacrifice of Christ Jesus in the Mass, the law of the prophets are fulfilled again in the highest. Therefore, while the Scriptures can be worthily proclaimed and heard in every corner of the universe, as they ought to be, it is only during the Liturgy of the Word at the memorial sacrifice where God's word is most worthily proclaimed and heard, and where hearing it immediately prepares us to most intimately receive His Only Begotten Word, Jesus Christ in the Sacrament of the Holy Eucharist.

When the People acclaim, **"The word of the Lord,"** they are shouting from the rooftops that when the Sacred Scriptures are read in the Mass, "God himself speaks to His People, and Christ, present in His word, proclaims the Gospel."[17] Therefore, the reader of the word participates in a ministerial role that is special to the royal priesthood alone.

Within the rhythm of prayer and confession in the Divine Symphony, the character of the readings is confessional, in that through them God bears witness and testimony of His love for His People. In this regard, the lector is not *in Persona Christi* as the Priest celebrant is, but the Lord is truly using that person as a vocal instrument in His Divine Symphony to proclaim His word to His People. He confesses the word to them in the vernacular; in their own language, so that they might hear God, rather than

---

[17] *GIRM*, II, 29.

hear babel. Moreover, not only is the lector a vocal instrument of God, but they are also in this moment a prophet of the Most High, and we receive a blessing at the hearing of their words, for, "Blessed is he who reads aloud the words of the prophecy, and blessed are those who hear, and who keep what is written therein; for the time is near."[18]

This particular movement in the Divine Symphony ought to cause us to harken back to an event during our Lord's earthly ministry, to that day when He stood up in the synagogue on the Sabbath and read from *Isaiah* 61:1-2, afterwards, "He closed the book, and gave it back to the attendant, and sat down."[19] Then with all eyes fixed on Him, He offered the shortest homily that any Catholic will ever hear, but should hear more often. He said, "Today this Scripture has been fulfilled in your hearing."[20] The news of the new jubilee year was very pleasing to the ears of those who heard Jesus' brief commentary on the reading of *Isaiah*. The text says, "And all spoke well of Him, and wondered at the gracious words which proceeded out of His mouth . . ."[21] Indeed, the word of God confessing and bearing witness and testimony of His love for His People truly does lift our spirits and brings us joy, but it must also convict us of our failings because His word is true. For, when Jesus then offered a second more challenging homily in response to their adulation and misunderstanding of how He Himself is the fulfillment of the prophet's words, ". . . all in the synagogue were filled with wrath. And they rose up and put Him out of the city, and led Him to the brow of the hill on which their city was built, that they might throw Him down headlong."[22]

---

[18] Rev. 1:3.
[19] Lk. 4:20.
[20] Lk. 4:21.
[21] Lk. 4:22.
[22] Lk. 4:29.

The emotions of joy and conviction are intended to naturally stir up in us whenever we listen to the readings while we are in intentional silence and reverent meditation. For, inasmuch as hearing the word of God provokes a significant amount of consternation and confliction of being *In*, yet so far, from Christ, it follows that by simply knowing that His word and promise is true, we cannot help but to cry out in adulation, **"Thanks be to God!"**

THE BIBLICAL READINGS

All of salvation history is summed up repeatedly in prayers and confessions of the Divine Symphony. From 'the Confiteor' to the 'Gloria in Excelsis Deo' to the Biblical readings, to the Eucharistic prayers, to the final blessing, all of salvation history and the covenant between God and man is summed up, prayed, and confessed. Therefore, it is fitting that the readings at Mass begin in the Old Testament where the record of salvation history begins. The primary exception of this practice comes during the season of Easter when Church tradition calls for the first reading to come from the *Book of Acts* so that all of our attention will be drawn to the mysteries of the Resurrection.

The Fathers of the Second Vatican Council taught that the "principal purpose to which the plan of the Old Covenant was directed was to prepare for the coming both of the Christ, the universal Redeemer, and of the messianic kingdom to announce this coming by prophecy,[23] and to indicate its meaning through various types.[24]"[25] In this way, with the lector serving as Divine Symphony's trumpet, the first reading doubly participates in that principal purpose by preparing us to receive the "principal witness of the life and teachings of the incarnate Word, our Savior"[26]

---

[23] Cf. Lk. 24:44, Jn. 5:39, 1 Pet. 1:10.
[24] Cf. 1 Cor. 10:11.
[25] *Dei Verbum*, 15.
[26] *Dei Verbum*, 18.

through the Gospel reading, and by preparing us to internally receive Him again through the Sacrament of the Holy Eucharist.

In the exordium of the first movement of the Divine Symphony, I briefly touched on the ontology of the periodic phrasing or the 'dialogue of persons' in the liturgy and how it finds its highest expression in the memorial sacrifice, but within that body of dialogues between God and man, the 'Responsorial Psalm' holds a chief position, because of its history amongst the People of God, to which J. A. Smith outlines:[27]

> Music occupied a prominent place in the ritual of the Jerusalem Temple in both pre- and post-exilic times. According to sources in the Old Testament, the Temple's musical organization followed traditions that reached back to King David,[28] who was regarded as having instituted them.[29] Performance of the music was entrusted mainly to Levites: they sang as a choir and played instruments.[30] Aaronites (priests) as well as Levites, however, might sound trumpets.[31] On occasion, processions round or into the Temple formed part of the ritual. These were conducted with the playing of instruments, including the playing of timbrels by young girls, and singing.[32] As far as the ordinal worshipers were concerned, their part in the Temple music was probably confirmed to the periodic interjection of acclamations such as 'Amen!', "Hallelujah!' and 'Glory!' while the Levites sang and played.[33]

---

[27] Smith, J.A. *Which Psalms Were Sung in the Temple*. Music and Letters. Oxford University Press. Vol. 71, No. 2 (May, 1990), 167.

[28] Cf. Ezra 3:10; Neh. 12:24, 36, 45; 2 Chr. 7:6, 23:18, 29:25-27, 35:15.

[29] Cf. Neh. 12:46; 1 Chr. 15:16-22, 23:1-6, 25:1-31; Sir. 47:8b-10.

[30] Cf. Ezra 3:10; Neh. 12:24, 27-29, 45; 1 Chr. 15:16-22, 27, 16:5, 41-42, 23:3-5, 25:1-7; 2 Chr. 5:12-13, 7:6, 29:25, 30:21. Josephus, *Antiquitates judaicae*. XX. 9:6. Mishnah, *Arakin* 2:3, 4, 6; *Bikurim* 3:4; *Midot* 2:5, 6; *Pesahim* 5:7; *Ros Hassana* 4:4; *Suka* 5:4; *Tamid* 5:6, 7:3, 4.

[31] Cf. Ezra 3:10a; Neh. 12:35, 41; 1 Chr. 15:24, 16:6; 2 Chr. 5:12-13, 7:6, 29:26; Sir. 50:16; Mishnah, *Arakin* 2:3; *Suka* 5:4; *Tamid* 7:3.

[32] Cf. Ps. 42:5, 48:13, 25-26, 118:27; Neh. 12:31-39; 1 Chr. 15:25-28; 1 Macc. 13:51; Josephus, *Bellum judaicum,* II, 15:4; Mishnah, *Bikurim* 3:4; *Suka* 4:1.

[33] Cf. Ps. 29:9, 106:48; Ezra 3:11c; 1 Chr. 16:38.

For both liturgy and private devotion, the *Psalms* serve as a collection of one hundred and fifty melodious dialogues with God that have been rhythmically embedded into salvation history. Yet, in being connected the Passion of Christ through the liturgy of Mass, the *Psalms* reach their beatific fulfillment. That is, all the hopes and promises of the *Psalms* are fulfilled in the *Ite, Missa est*, and the dialogues with God that these melodies propose reach their perfect joy there, in His quad Presence.

In the Divine Symphony's rhythm of prayer and confession, the first, second, and Gospel readings are melodies of God confessing His love for His People. Yet, 'the Responsorial' serves a different role. When we sing or chant 'the Responsorial,' we become God's chorus in union with the heavenly hosts and angels. After the minister proclaims each stanza of the Psalm, we acclaim and joyfully confess God's great work. If every Catholic knew the blessing that comes from telling God how great and marvelous His love and works are, the world would be able to hear us from outside of the Church building. They would be driving past in their cars and hear that Catholics love their God. To be certain, it is truly a colossal shame that Muslims understand this concept much better than Catholics. Draw near to any Mosque during their times of prayer, you always hear Muslims shouting 'Allahu akbar' (Allah is the greatest), but from 'the Confiteor', to 'the Gloria in Excelsis Deo' to 'the Responsorial' to 'the Creed', everything that the Catholic confesses is a mere whisper. What a tragedy, and what a missed opportunity to give witness about the great glory our God!

The second liturgical reading is always drawn from one of the twenty-four letters or treatises in the New Testament and is purposed to assist the People in their pilgrimage on Earth by offering instruction, consolation, encouragement, chastisement, warning, and advice on dispute resolution. In ministering God's words to His People, the lector would do very well to attend to the seriousness of the Holy Spirit in these matters, while also striking a tone and cadence of hope.

Unfortunately, it is the tendency of too many during this melody of the Divine Symphony to hear it is as being nothing more than the final crescendo to the climax of this rite; the Gospel reading. In part, that is true; beginning with the First reading, there has been a gradual and steady increase in the mysteries of the word, but it is also true that the People of God would do well in their hearing to receive these letters and treatises as a collection of some of the earliest Apostolic homilies in the Catholic Church. For, these are some of the earliest reflections on the salvific mystery of Christ Jesus, and some of the earliest guides and exhortations on how we ought to live in this world as Christians. To overlook and to not receive the beauty of this short melody is make our accompanying acclamation, **"Thanks be to God,"** very hollow and insubstantial.

After the Second reading, the priesthood of the Baptized joins the ordained priesthood in giving full attention to the matter by returning to their standing prayer posture to offer an acclamation to God by singing 'Alleluia' or another chant that is led by the choir or a cantor. "An acclamation of this kind constitutes a rite or act in itself, by which the gathering of the faithful welcomes and greets the Lord who is about to speak to them in the Gospel and profess their faith by means of the chant."[34]

During the acclamation, the Deacon will bow profoundly before the Priest and ask for a blessing, saying, **"Your blessing, Father."** To this petition, the Priest replies in a low voice, **"May the Lord be in your heart and on your lips, that you may proclaim His Gospel worthily and well, in the name of the Father and of the Son and of the Holy Spirit."** The Deacon then signs himself with the Sign of the Cross and replies, **"Amen."** Should a Deacon not

---

[34] *GIRM*, III, 62.

be present, the Priest, bowing before the altar, says quietly, **"Cleanse my heart and my lips, almighty God, that I may worthily proclaim your holy Gospel."**

The Deacon or Priest then proceeds to the ambo, accompanied, if appropriate, by ministers with incense and candles. It is there that he offers for a second time to the People of God the blessing, **"The Lord be with you,"** to which they respond again in like blessing, **"And with your spirit."** As in the first movement, and with the next three, this repeated short periodic phrasing is to serve as a signal to the People that there has been a liturgical escalation in the principal matter of the Mass, which is to make Christ Jesus present to His People.

A more extended and arguably more beautiful version of the Priest's petition to God is found in the Tridentine Rite; **"Cleanse my heart and my lips, O Almighty God, Who didst cleanse the lips of the prophet Isaiah with burning coal; through Thy gracious mercy so purify me that I may worthily proclaim Thy holy Gospel. Through Christ our Lord. Amen. Grant, O Lord, Thy Blessing. May the Lord be in my heart and on my lips that I may worthily, and fitting proclaim His Gospel. Amen."** The higher beauty of this prayer is not found in it merely being longer, but, rather, in that it petitions God specifically according to His word. Essentially, the Priest is saying, 'Lord do unto me as you had done to your prophets before me.' Indeed, there is no faster way to get God to act in your life than by calling upon Him to be faithful to His own word.

While the display of the Book of the Gospels plays a much more prominent role in the Divine Liturgy of the Byzantine Rite, the Priest's prayers over the Deacon and the responses of the Baptized priesthood are similar. The main point of departure between these rites is in regard to the Priest's 'Prayer Before the Gospel,' which he says before the Holy Table and immediately prior to the Deacon's blessing: "O Master, Lover of Mankind,[35] shine forth within our hearts the pure light of Your Divine knowledge.[36] Open the eyes of our mind that we may understand the teachings of Your Gospel. Instill in us also the fear of Your blessed commandments, so that, having trampled[37] all carnal passions,[38] we may lead a spiritual life, both thinking and doing those things which are pleasing to You. For You, O Christ God, are the enlightenment of our souls and bodies;[39] and to You, we send up glory, together with your Father, Who is without beginning,[40] and with Your all-holy, good, and life-creating Spirit,[41] now and ever, and to the ages of ages. Amen." Rooted deeply in the Scriptures, this prayer asks God to bestow a special grace upon the hearers so that a new metanoia might occur upon their hearing of the Gospel.

Regardless of the liturgical rite, the elevation in tempo and the degree of participation in this second movement of the Divine Symphony should make us all aware that the steady crescendo is ready to climax. From the standing in attention, to the blessing of the Deacon, to the procession of the Book of the Gospels, to signing of our head, mouth, and heart with the 'Sign of the Cross', and to the scent and smoke of incense; everything about the present transformation in activity should alert all of our senses and our faith that something tremendous is about to happen. The meaning of this transformation in activity is that a higher transformation in activity should occur in our lives upon hearing Gospel of Christ Jesus.

---

[35] Cf. Tit. 3:4.
[36] Cf. 2 Cor. 4:6.
[37] Cf. 1 Pet. 2:11.
[38] Cf. 1 Jn. 3:22.
[39] Cf. Jn. 1:9.
[40] Cf. Isa. 9:6.
[41] Cf. Jn. 6:63.

In a symphony orchestra, the theme of the second movement will consist of several progressive variations, from a modification of the theme itself, embellishments, differing instrumentations, and etcetera. Altogether, the purpose of which is to capture and to hold the hearer's attention and to, thereby, successfully matriculate them deeper into drama and towards the next movement.

In this way, musical arrangements and rituals have a great deal in common. As with all rituals, especially the liturgy of the memorial sacrifice, the intended purpose of the arrangements and actions are to convey a significant and profound meaning that will be permanently impressed upon the mind of the participant or hearer. Therefore, whenever the arrangement of the ritual dramatically changes, just as it does at this point in the Liturgy of the Word, it is vitally important to attend to the signs and what they are pointing to. In the instant case, all signs are pointing to the primacy of the Gospel of Christ Jesus and how His life was purposed to transform ours. As Saint Athanasius wrote in his *Discourse Against the Arians*, "For this reason did He assume a body created and human; so that, having renewed it as its Creator, He might deify it in Himself, and thus might introduce all of us in that likeness into the kingdom of heaven." Then again, but more succinctly, in his *On the Incarnation of the Word of God and Against the Arians*, he wrote, "Accordingly, the Son of God became Son of Man, so that the sons of man, that is, of Adam, might become sons of God." This pointing to the process of divinization that we find in the Liturgy of the Word will be immediately fulfilled in the upcoming Liturgy of the Eucharist.

Another reason why we stand at attention at this moment in the Divine Symphony is in response to the transition that is occurring, where we move from the apostolic letters and treatises to the Gospels of Jesus Christ. While all of the Scriptures were composed under the inspiration of the Holy Spirit, the fathers of the Second Vatican Council called it, "...common knowledge that among all the Scriptures, even those of the New Testament, the Gospels have a special preeminence, and rightly so, for they are the principal witness for the life and teaching of the incarnate Word, our savior."[42] Along with all of the other associative symbolism peculiar to the Gospel reading, it is given its final distinction from the other readings with the Priest's or Deacon's closing acclamation, **"The Gospel of the Lord,"** to which the Baptized priesthood says, **"Praise to you, Lord Jesus Christ."**

That closing periodic phrasing after the Gospel reading is the capstone to the tempo of the second movement of the Divine Symphony, and historically the Catholic liturgies have always found the most beautiful words to note this apogee of the Liturgy of the Word. In the Syriac Maronite Rite, the Celebrant says, **"This is the truth. Peace be with you,"** to which the congregation responds, **"Praise and blessings to Jesus Christ for His living word to us."** In the liturgy of Saint John Chrysostom of the Byzantine Rite, the Priest says, **"Praise be with you who have proclaimed the Holy Gospel,"** and the People respond, **"Glory to You, O Lord, glory to You."** The common theme between these periodic phrasings is that we have been blessed beyond measure to have received the words of God, and we are eternally grateful to Him for having given us His word. After the Gospel reading has concluded in the Tridentine Rite, the Baptized Priesthood offers, **"Praise be to Thee, O Christ,"** and in response, the Priest prays, "By the words of the Gospel may our sins be blotted out."

The Novus Ordo Rite borrows from this closing petition of the Tridentine when the Priest or Deacon kisses the Book of the Gospel and then says quietly, **"Through the words of the Gospel may our sins be wiped away."** This second sacramental absolu-

---

[42] *Dei Verbum*, 18.

tion (after the Penitential Rite) is evidence that People's reception and response to the Gospel has opened them up to receive the graces needed to worthily receive in their mouths what they have just heard a taste of with their ears.

While some may think it is unfortunate that the People of the Novus Ordo cannot audibly hear their Priest intercede for them in this way, it is true that neither could the Jews hear their High Priest intercede and atone for their sins while he was away in the Holy of Holies. "Likewise, the Spirit helps us in our weakness; for we do not know how to pray as we ought, but the Spirit Himself intercedes for us with sighs too deep for words."[43] On the contrary, it is not as vital for the People to hear what the Priest says in intercession, inasmuch as it is vital for them to know that he is interceding for them. For, what is sacred and mysterious is always veiled and enveloped in God's silent presence. "In the liturgy, the chalice is veiled; the ciborium and the tabernacle are covered with a veil when they contain the Real Presence. Silence is an acoustic veil that protects the mystery. Do we not automatically lower our voice to say the most important things, words of love?"[44] Moreover, these secret prayers of the Priest during the Divine Symphony are opportunities for the God's ever pervasive odor of silence to fall upon His People. In this brief silence, they are made aware again of His ever-embracing Presence.

If it is true that only silence can lead us beyond the limits and temptations of words, and into the mystery of worship in spirit and truth, then it is also true that the *Ite, Missa est* is most like the Incarnation in its facilities to take our prayers and confessions of acquiescence and, in silence, bring us the fruit of eternal life. For, no one heard the sound of the Incarnation, no more than we hear the sound of bread and wine becoming the Flesh and Blood of

---

[43] Rom. 8:26.
[44] *The Power of Silence*, 242.

God. Furthermore, it confesses the limits of human noise if rattling of bells is the best that we can do to stir the imagination into a moment so Divine, mysterious, and consequential.

THE HOMILY

As was discussed at the beginning of this exordium, in the example of the Levites (Priests) helping the People understand the book of the law that Ezra was reading,[45] and with Jesus' very short Sabbath day homily following a reading from the prophet Isaiah in a synagogue in His hometown of Nazareth,[46] it has long been the tradition of the ordained ministry to explain God's word to His People. In finding that the homily "is necessary for the nurturing of the Christian life,"[47] the Divine Symphony brings to fulfillment this liturgical praxis.

Again, one of the earliest attestations to this subject in the second movement of the Divine Symphony comes from chapter sixty-seven ('Weekly Worship of the Christians') of Saint Justin Martyr's *First Apology*, written between 152 and 155 A.D.:

> And on the day called Sunday, all who live in cities or in the country gather together to one place, and the memoirs of the apostles or the writings of the prophets are read, as long as time permits; then, when the reader has finished, he who presides over those gathered admonishes and challenge them to imitate these beautiful things.[48]

The Fathers of the Second Vatican Council in their *Sacrosanctum Concilium* (Constitution on the Sacred Liturgy), expressed the essentiality of the homily in this way:

> By means of the homily the mysteries of the faith and the guiding principles of the Christian life are expounded from the sacred text, during

---

[45] Cf. Neh. 8:7-8.
[46] Cf. Lk. 4:21.
[47] *GIRM*, III, 65.
[48] St. Justin, *Apol.* 1, 67.

the course of the liturgical year; the homily, therefore, is to be highly esteemed as part of the liturgy itself; in fact, at those Masses which are celebrated with the assistance of the people on Sundays and feasts of obligation, it should not be omitted except for a serious reason.[49]

Therefore, being that the homily is purposed to be pedagogical, it belongs to the teaching ministry of the Church (i.e., the Bishop), and to those who are ordained to participate in their ministry to deliver it. As the Twelve Apostles, along with Paul and their successors acted as a collegial body and exercised the normative oversight of teaching, judging, prophetic warning and applying the Gospel, so too are their successors today called and guided by the Holy Spirit to their preaching and by the example of their own lives to impart the saving truth of Jesus Christ to others. "First among those who assist the Bishops in their ministry of teaching are those ordained for this very purpose, the Priests."[50] Inasmuch as this principal task of the Priest is to execute the teaching ministry of the bishop on the local level, it also extends to "parish religious education programs and other forms of pastoral ministry,"[51] it is only in that uniquely liturgical opportunity where the Priest and Deacon have at their disposal every day of the week to impart to the attentive People the saving truth of Jesus Christ.

In this regard, the Priest and Deacon would do well always to remember these four things; first, the tradition of expounding upon the Scriptures that they are connected to; second, that teaching the Gospel is also living it in the example of their own lives; third, that this teaching ministry belongs not to them, but to the Bishop, and that it should, therefore, be exercised in union

---

[49] Sacrosanctum concilium, 52.
[50] *The Teaching Ministry of the Diocesan Bishop*, National Conference of Catholic Bishops. 1992. 8.
[51] *The Teaching Ministry of the Diocesan Bishop*, 9.

with the mission of the Bishop; and forth, that any words used that do not connect the readings with salvific mission of Christ Jesus are wasted words.

For their part, the People of God would do well to remember these two things; first, that they are called to sit and listen to the Priest in silence because he is at this moment exercising a sacred office through which we might encounter the Presence of God in our lives even more deeply; second, that this is the only subject during the Divine Symphony in which the Priest's words are not protected from error. Meaning that at nearly every other moment during the Mass, the Priest has only said what Mother Church gave him to say; he never spoke His own words, but Hers, which protected him and all of Her children from error, and which were beneficial for their salvation. Yet, for the next several minutes, the Priest will speak many of his own words. Therefore, the People of God would do well during this subject to attend the Priest's words, similar to how the Jews of Beroea attended to words of Paul and Silas,[52] by receiving the word with all eagerness and examining the Scriptures daily to see if these things are consistent with what has been revealed by Christ Jesus and His Church.

Another simultaneous great joy and great disappointment in being Catholic is learning that the teaching office of the Bishop is united to the Holy Spirit, and our Priest participates in that sacred office, but his ability to communicate the saving truth of Jesus Christ without any demonstration of qualities that demand us to lean forward, be drawn into the beauty, or yearn for more, is too often very poor.

My first time ever hearing a Catholic homily was extraordinary. While, heretofore, I had been used to being thoroughly entertained and motivated by the Protestant style sermons, the

---

[52] Cf. Acts 17:10-12.

clear homiletic teaching offered by Father Patrick Toner that January in 2006 far exceeded my expectations. It was not that Father Pat was a great orator or that the pitch of his voice was heavenly. While the quality of his voice was good, it is not what caused me to remember his homily for years thereafter. Rather, it was because he very carefully, artfully, and simply highlighted the readings of the Mass and then explained them. He didn't need to add any personal stories or cute little anecdotes to make us laugh. He didn't need to leave the ambo to engage us so that we might be more attentive. He just commented on the word of God in a way that allowed the People of God to imagine how we might reconcile ourselves to God through His word. That simple exercise in sound homiletics was perfect for me.

Oh, how I wish the Lord didn't spoil me during those early formative years, but how much I appreciate the fact that I may not have converted if those homilies didn't satisfy my thirst to drink from the well of God's word. It is my hope and prayer that all Priests would use their homily to soundly teach from the reading to offer Christ Jesus' salvific truth in union with the Church. Just to do that one thing would be abundantly enough.

THE CREED OR PROFESSION OF FAITH

In the liturgical rhythm of prayers and confessions in the Divine Symphony, the Creed offers the final opportunity in the Liturgy of the Word to confess our belief in the Triune God. Its positioning in the liturgy gives it the taste of being something of a summation of the readings, and as a preface to the Liturgy of the Eucharist. Indeed, all the confessions found in the Creed sum up what God has revealed about Himself and about His work to fulfill in us the desire of Eve; that is, to be like God. Also, the Creed, in treating the nature of God, addresses and points to the central theme of the Divine Symphony primarily; that is, the work of deification – becoming like God. Therefore, when we confess the

Creed, we are confessing our belief in the Divine nature of God and His work to conform us to that nature, through our Lord Jesus Christ.

The creeds pronounced at the Councils of Nicaea and Constantinople are not the earliest instances of the declarative statements by the fathers about the nature, personhood, life, and works of the Triune Godhead, but they do provide a well-organized place to begin the discussion about what the Church believes about the nature of God and His Church.

The creed of Nicaea, representing a joint effort of the Fathers of the Council,[53] was the first time in history that the Catholic Church officially spoke on the preexistent nature of the Church, immediately prior to their announcement of anathemas:

> We believe in One God, the Father Almighty, Creator of all things visible and invisible; and in One Lord Jesus Christ, the Son of God, begotten as the only -begotten of the Father, that is from the essence [ousia] of the Father, God from God, Light from Light, true God form true God, begotten, not created, consubstantial [homo-ousios] with the Father, through Whom [i.e. the Son] all things were made, both in Heaven and Earth; Who for us men and for our salvation came down and was incarnate, was made Man; Who suffered and rose again on the third day, ascended into Heaven, and shall come again to judge the living and the dead; **and in the Holy Spirit.** – But those who say, **'There was a time when He [the Son] was not,** and 'He was not before he was made;' and 'He was made out of nothing,' or 'He is of another substance' or 'essence,' or 'The Son of God is created,' or

---

[53] The fathers are not in wholly agreement on who was the principal author of the Creed of Nicaea. According to St. Basil it was authored by Hermongenes of Caesarea in Cappadocia, later a Bishop, who was at the council in the capacity of Deacon and who was secretary wrote the agreed upon Creed and read it aloud on June 19, 325. Yet, according to St. Hilary, it was Athanasius who authored the final Creed in response to the Arian heresy, but Athanasius, who was in a best position to know the author, states that Ossius of Cordova was its principal contributor. *The Faith of the Early Fathers. Volume I*, 281. Laux, John. *Church History*. Tan, Charlotte, North Carolina. 1989. 112. Print.

'changeable,' or 'alterable'— they are condemned by the holy catholic and apostolic Church.

The first of the five opposition statements ('There was a time when He was not') is primarily being asserted here to defend the Holy Spirit against claims that He was created and not truly God in nature and being.[54] In this first statement is also found the argument for the preexistent nature of the Church. Being that the Church proceeds from the life and mission of the Holy Spirit, we can rightly join the Creed in saying that there was never a time when the Church was not.

Attributed to the First Council of Constantinople by the Council of Chalcedon in A.D. 451, the Nicene-Constantinople Creed actually predates the A.D. 381 council by at least seven to twenty years and was recited in its entirety by Epiphanius of Salamis in his A.D. 374 *Ancoratus.*[55] Both of these creeds omit nothing from the Creed of Nicaea but add more to Second Person of the Holy Trinity (e.g. "according to the Scriptures," "and is seated at the right of the Father," "in glory," "whose kingdom there will be no end"). Most especially, they have a great deal to say about the preexisting and supernatural nature of the Church in the Holy Spirit:

> "And in the Holy Spirit, the Lord, the Giver of life, who is proceeding from the Father, who together with the Father and the Son is adored and glorified, who spoke through the prophets. In one holy, catholic, and apostolic Church; we confess one Baptism for the remission of sins, and we await the resurrection of the dead and a life of the age to come. Amen."

---

[54] The Manicheans denied that the Old Testament was from God, and claimed that the Persian Mani himself was the Holy Spirit (but not Divine). Priscillianism and Montanism both denied that the Holy Spirit spoke through the Old Covenant prophets.

[55] *The Faith of the Early Fathers. Volume I.* The Liturgical Press, Collegeville, Minnesota. 1970. 398.

What the Creed offers here is a construct in three sections by which the Church instructs the world to know the triune nature, personhood, life, and works of the Father, Son, and Holy Spirit. In regard to the Father, the first thing we need to know about Him is the same thing Jews knew about YHWH from the first paragraph of the Shema, "Here, Israel, the Lord is our God, the Lord is One."[56] This is a fundamental expression of our faith and belief in the nature of God; that He is neither subordinate nor divided – He is one. That this one God is rightly called Father Almighty bespeaks of eternal primacy above all of His household and of His creative power to bring life where there was none.

Out of this nature of unity and personhood, best described as Eternal Father, His life and works springs forth, which He desires to share by bringing to life and in love those things that are both visible and invisible; the first of which is His Only-begotten Son – begotten in His oneness, and, therefore, rightly called One Lord Jesus Christ, the Son of God. There is nothing new about the nature of the Son that is not of the Father. For, He is eternal ("before all ages"), Light from Light, God from God (or Very God of Very God), truly from the God, rather than being created ("Begotten, not made), and, therefore, truly of the same substance ("consubstantial") with the Father, but distinct in personhood because the Son is not the Father ("by whom all things were made").

The following disambiguation of this second section of the Creed can also explain how and why only Divine love flows from out of the nature of God. For, out of this nature and unity with His Eternal Father and personhood of being the Son of God, comes forth His life and works, which is for the salvation of man for whom He came down from Heaven, and was incarnate of the Holy Spirit and the Virgin Mary, as was made man; and was crucified also for us under Pontius Pilate for our sake, and suffered

---

[56] Dt. 6:4-9.

and was buried and rose again on the third day, in accordance with the Scriptures, and ascended into Heaven, and now sits at the right hand of the Father. In continuance with His life and works, He shall come again with glory to judge the living and the dead, and His kingdom will participate in His eternal nature.

Before we discuss the third and final section, let us recapitulate the formula of the Creed that has thus far been revealed. The previous two instructions about the Father and the Son both informed us about the names by which the first two persons of the Holy Trinity are rightfully called; Father Almighty and Lord Jesus Christ. They also highlighted the origin and personhood of the Father and Son; God is one – He has no source of being, and Jesus Christ is His Only-begotten Son. Next, the Creed instructs us about the life and works of the Father and the Son; God is the creator, and the Son is for the salvation of man.

With this pattern in place, it would then seem to, therefore, follow that the final paragraph will also instruct us on the name, origin, personhood, life, and works of the third person of the Holy Trinity. It would not logically follow that the Creed would include a fourth person or some other entity that is somehow not in relation to the one nature of God.

On the contrary, the final section of the Creed begins: "And in the Holy Spirit, the Lord, the Giver of life, who is proceeding from the Father, who together with the Father and the Son is adored and glorified."[57] The section alone follows the established pattern in the Creed by addressing the name by which the Third Person is rightfully called, Holy Spirit (Ghost); His origin and personhood springs forth from the one Divine substance of the Father and the Son, out of which He proceeds and through which He shares in glory and adoration.

---

[57] Latin version of the Nicene-Constantinople Creed and the Tridentine teaching of the procession of the Holy Spirit, "who proceeds from the Father AND the Son . . ."

The remainder of the third section of Creed continues to follow the pattern by instructing us about the life and works of the Holy Spirit, which is to unify and gather the people of God into the one communion through which Jesus Christ effects His work of salvation. This gathering can uniquely be found whenever and wherever the Holy Spirit spoke through the prophets and finally culminated in the One, Holy, Catholic, and Apostolic Church. It is through this covenantal gathering of the Holy Spirit by which the People cooperate with Jesus Christ in their salvation by receiving one Baptism for the forgiveness of sins, which prepares them and gives them hope for the resurrection of the dead and the life in the age to come.

These two early creeds are more than simple confessions recited at the Sacrifice of the Mass. Rather, they are the resolutions of the Fathers of the Church in response to the Arian and Neo-Arian heresies concerning the origin, nature, life, and works of the three persons of the Holy Trinity, and it is fitting that Catholic Church should be included in the Creeds as part of the life of the Holy Spirit, "For where the Church is, there also is God's Spirit; where God's Spirit is, there is the Church and every grace."[58] It is just as impossible to speak of the Church without speaking of Christ, as it is to speak of Christ without speaking of His Church because the former participates in the nature of the latter.

It is most certainly true that the Nicaea-Constantinople Creed disclosed in the most explicit language possible at the time that the Church is both a Divine and human institution that consists of two natures; one Divine and one human, who is being made like the Divine; a nature that has descended to save and a nature that is necessarily being saved to ascend. For this reason, it is essential for the Catholic to know the history and theology

---

[58] St Irenaeus, *Adv. Haeres.* 3, 24, 1.

of the Creed so that when they confess it, they will also connect it to the principal matter of the Divine Symphony. That is, the Creed is defending and proclaiming the nature of God that the *Ite, Missa est* is preparing and facilitating the People to be one with. Therefore, to not know how the Church understands the nature of God, is not to understand why you are even at the memorial sacrifice in the first place.

While some of the liturgies of the Eastern rites do exclude the *filioque* (i.e., who proceeds from the Father **and the Son/Filioque procedit**), it has been the common tradition for centuries in Churches that are in union with Church of Peter and Paul to call the People of God to recite together these earliest dogmas and essential confessions of the Church that teach us what it means to be a Catholic, and, thereby, ready and worthy to participate ever more deeply in the process of divinization.

THE UNIVERSAL PRAYER OR PRAYER OF THE FAITHFUL OR BIDDING PRAYERS

As the Creed serves as the confessional response to the readings and homily, now enters the Universal Prayer of the People of God "to respond in some sense to the Word of God which they have received in faith, and exercising the office of their baptismal Priesthood,"[59] offering prayers for the salvation of all. In chapters sixty-five and sixty-seven ('Weekly Worship of the Christians') of Saint Justin Martyr's *First Apology*, he offered this commentary about the ancient practice of the Universal Prayer:

> Then we all rise together . . . in order that we may offer hearty prayers in common for ourselves and for the baptized [illuminated] person, and for all others in every place, that we may be counted worthy, now that we have learned the truth, by our works also to be found good citizens

---

[59] *GIRM*, III, 69.

and keepers of the commandments, so that we may be saved with an everlasting salvation.[60]

Heretofore, the intercessions of the Priest and the prayers of the People had only been directed towards the graces of God that are needed to receive the Holy Eucharist worthily. Now, after hearing the readings, the homily, and confessing in the Creed the summation of those things, the People are God have been compelled to act accordingly to the truth and offer intercessory prayers for each other and for all; begging the Lord who is "able for all time to save those who draw near to God through Him, since He always lives to make intercession for them."[61] These are intercessory prayers being offered by the Priest, Deacon, cantor, or reader are so vital that we are called to stand in attention to hear them, and to express our agreement with the prayer "either by an invocation said in common after each intention or by praying in silence."[62]

It is true that petitions offered during 'the Prayer of the Faithful' can oftentimes be quite audacious, and for that reason I have wondered whether most of the People of God who are gathered at the memorial sacrifice even believe that God will do what they are asking Him to do, or when they affirm those petitions, saying "Amen" or "Lord Hear our Prayer," are they really counter-affirming in their heads, "I hope for the best with that" or "God I don't really think you are interested in our concerns, but thanks for hearing them anyway. That's so swell of you." I think that too many Catholic Christians fall tremendously short in truly believing that the more audacious their prayers are, the more audacious their faith needs to be.

---

[60] *GIRM*, III, 67.
[61] Heb. 7:25.
[62] *GIRM*, III, 71.

Intercessory prayer has four character marks; 1) it is selfless, 2) audacious, 3) courageous, and 4) full of faith. These four marks combine to indicate that intercessory prayer is a sacrifice in that it places one's own life at harm for the wellbeing of the other. In this way, intercessory prayer and living as a Christian in this world are symbiotic. For us to successfully enter into this sacrificial venture together is to place our feet into the well-grounded footprints of the Communion of Saints and to pray as selflessly, audaciously, courageously, and faithfully as they prayed; trusting in the magnanimous mercy of God. We should always call to memory how selfless, audacious, and courageous Abraham's faith was when he interceded for the righteous people of Sodom; asking first if the Lord found fifty righteous people, then down to just thirty, and finally if there were just ten righteous people in Sodom, if He would have spared that wicked city. Abraham is the model of what the Church teaches, in saying, "in intercession, he who prays looks "not only to his own interests but also to the interest of others," even to the point of praying for those who do him harm."[63] The *Catechism of the Catholic Church* continues:[64]

The first Christian communities lived this form of fellowship intensely.[65] Thus the Apostle Paul gives them a share in his ministry of preaching the Gospel[66] but also intercedes for them.[67] The intercession of Christians recognizes no boundaries: "for all men, for kings and all who are in high positions," for persecutors for the salvation of those who reject the Gospel.[68]

---

[63] CCC. 2635.
[64] CCC. 2636.
[65] Cf. Acts 12:5, 20:26, 21:5; 2 Cor. 9:14.
[66] Cf. Eph. 6:18-20; Col. 4:3-4; 1 Thess. 5:25.
[67] Cf. 2 Thess. 1:11; Col. 1:3; Phil. 1:3-4.
[68] 1 Tim. 2:1; cf. rom. 12:14, 10:1.

Along with the introduction to the Mass and the Homily, the Universal Prayer is the third and final pause in the Divine Symphony that allows for the liberal insertion of words that are either harmonious or discordant with the orthodoxy of the faith.

As with you, I have also seen the beautiful and unselfish side that this prayer of the People of God presents many times. For example, when I worked on the Diocese of Columbus Ohio 'Accompanying Returning Citizens with Hope' committee to build a culture of concern and ministry for the imprisoned and those returning home from prison. By working with the Priests and Deacons in the diocese, we inspired many of them to either preach a homily about the Christian duty towards the imprisoned and/or to insert prayers for the imprisoned and those affected by mass incarceration into their 'Universal Prayer' on Sundays. In my own parish at the time, Saint Matthew the Apostle in Gahanna, Ohio, I heard one of those prayers, and it felt terrific to hear everyone say in response, "Lord, hear our prayer." As with others who have traveled around and experienced many different parishes, I have also seen an ugly side of the 'Universal Prayer,' when it has included ideas that are heretical to our faith, and when it has been used as a weapon to attack a sitting President of the United States personally.

Along with always remembering that the Sacrifice of the Mass is the highest prayer of the Church and that it is a sacred confession of faith, we must never forget the Mass belongs to God alone for the perfect benefit of His People. Therefore, to hijack any part of the Divine Symphony for selfish motives is to steal from God, from neighbor, from self, and from the Church.

The Third Movement
of
The Divine Symphony

EXORDIUM TO THE LITURGY OF THE EUCHARIST

Just as we experienced in the Liturgy of the Word, with the transformation in activity with the procession of the Book of the Gospels, the signing our head, mouth, and heart of 'the Sign of the Cross', the scent and smoke of incense, and etcetera, the present transformation in activity in the Liturgy of the Eucharist should again alert all of our senses and our faith that something even more tremendous is about to happen. For, the altar is changing form, the ministers are placing the corporeal, the purificator, the chalice, the pall, and the Missal on it, and the Priest no longer stands away from the altar, but, instead, stands immediately before it.

Following the second movement of the Divine Symphony, enters the third movement, which in the classical symphony era was usually a minuet (based on the old courtly dance), then made popular in the courts of King Louis XIV. When not having to contend with dancers, the originally short ¾ pace of the minuets kept speeding up over time, and it was eventually replaced by the scherzo (i.e., joke or play), which were composed as livelier and often lighthearted tunes. Joseph Haydn (1732 – 1809), the Father of the Symphonic form and of the String Quartet,[1] and a Catholic who would often employ the aid of praying the rosary to help him compose his symphonies, made the minuet standard equipment in his symphonies. Like the sonata form, which Mozart oftentimes preferred as a third movement, the minuet oftentimes consists of three sections: a minuet or scherzo played by the orchestra, followed by a trio played by a trio of instruments, and closing with a minuet or scherzo played by the orchestra again.

As a dance, the minuet (from the French, meaning "small") became vastly popular in the European ballrooms of high society from about 1650 to 1750. The key distinguishing features of the dance are the choreographed floor movements, the courting interplay between the dancers, and the stylized bows and curtsies to partners and spectators.

The idea of parts of the Liturgy of the Eucharist being a type of minuet in both song and dance is not something that is peculiar to the African and Indian Catholics whose worship of God not only includes the word, song, bodily movements like the rest of the Universal Church, but also includes ritualized dance, which is "clearly distinct from the martial dance and from the amorous dance,"[2] because such forms of dance for them during 'the Entrance' and 'the Offertory' still reflects religious values and a manifestation of their love for God.

In the more somber Tridentine and Novus Ordo rites, the minuet is found in the pace of the offertory chant and in the rhythm of the activities; all of which serves the same purpose to point the People of God to the purpose of the Liturgy of the Eu-

---

[1] Rosen, Charles. *The classical style: Haydn, Mozart, Beethoven* (2nd ed.). Norton. New York. 1997. 43-54.

[2] *The Religious Dance, an Expression of Spiritual Joy.* Notitiae. 11 (1975) 202-205.

charist, which is to divinize us. Whereas the first movement prepared us to receive the written and edible Word of God worthily, and the second movement actuated a deeper metanoia in our heart by revealing God's transformative words to us, now enters the third movement to make us like God, by physical digesting the Body, Blood, Soul, and Divinity of Jesus Christ.

From 'the Preparation of the Gifts' to 'the Communion Feast', the dramatically increased level of participation of the People of God during every subject of this rite points to the dangerous beautiful reality of our salvation; that "the God who created you without your cooperation, will not save you without your cooperation."[3] In that way, this real dialogue between the whole person of Jesus Christ and the whole person of the Baptized at Mass, is also characteristic of the choreographed and restrained dances found in the European courtly society.

This cooperative participation and courtly dance between God and man for the sake of the divinization of the latter is yet another sign that the Sacrifice of the Mass is wholly other to the world. For, there is little dancing with the will God outside of His Divine Symphony, but there is a great deal of fighting against it. On the contrary, in the cacophony of the world, we are like Jacob; we are Israel in all that we do for most of our days is wrestle and struggle with God,[4] which helps our will to be necessarily reconciled to His. What the Liturgy of the Eucharist offers in contrast to the world is a salient and perfect choreography and interplay between the Creator and His creations so that He might voluntarily give them what Eve attempted to steal; that is, a partaking of His life. Indeed, the Holy Mass is the only place on Earth where God essentially says, 'Come! Cooperate in my life by taking my life into you.'

---

[3] St. Augustine, *Sermo* 169, 13 (Pl 38, 923).
[4] Cf. Gen. 32:22-31.

THE PREPARATION (THE OFFERTORY)

As our salvation is sustained by our participation in the loving and sacrificial offering of God's only Begotten Son, so too does the Sacrament of Eternal Life take rise within a participative economy. Beginning with the 'Preparation of Gifts,' through which we are called to offer a loving and sacrificial offering of our own, our witness is that the God who created us without our co-operation, will not save us without our cooperation.[5]

Noted in the English translation of the Roman Missal, "It is desirable that the faithful express their participation by making an offering, bringing forward bread and wine for the celebration of the Eucharist and perhaps other gifts to relieve the needs of the Church and of the poor." In chapter sixty-seven of this *First Apology*, Saint Justin Martyr attested to this 'The Offertory' practice in the memorial sacrifice:

> There is then brought to the president of the brethren bread and a cup of wine mixed with water; and he taking them, gives praise and glory to the Father of the universe, through the name of the Son and of the Holy Ghost, and offers thanks at considerable length for our being counted worthy to receive these things at His hands.[6]

While 'The Offertory' is clearly attested to by Saint Justin Martyr as late as the mid-second century as being a part of the third movement of the Divine Symphony, the very act of making a sacrificial offering to God is arguably something that we always have known to do according to our human nature. We were created for offering. Even with Adam, who did not seem to have voluntarily offered his own rib, was tremendously pleased with what God did with his sacrifice; exclaiming, "This one, at last, is bone of my bones and flesh of my flesh; This one shall be called

---

[5] Cf. St. Augustine, *Sermo* 169, 13 (Pl 38, 923).
[6] St. Justin, *Apol.* 1, 67.

'woman,' for out of man this one has been taken."[7] That God took the best of Adam and gave what was good and beneficial of it back him, and Adam was thankful for it, is a type of offertory and a type of eucharist. Abel offering to God his best; "the firstlings of his flock,"[8] was offertory in that it required thought, effort, and sacrifice, and for this, God was pleased. While Cain, simply picking from fruits that had either fallen to the ground from trees or grew up from the soil required very little thought, effort, or sacrifice. Melchizedek, king of Salem, bringing out bread and wine to Abraham and blessing him was offertory and eucharistic; to which Abraham returned, in like sacrifice, by giving Melchizedek a tenth of everything he owned.[9] From the outset of salvation history it is clear that we were created for *todah* (Heb. meaning 'thank offering'). We were created eucharistic to be a eucharistic people.

Even our human bodies were created to always be in a mode of offering. In his 16th of January 1980 General Audience, Pope John Paul II said:

> One can say that created by Love, that is, endowed in their being with masculinity and femininity, both are "naked," because they are *free with the very freedom of the gift*. This freedom lies exactly at the basis of the spousal meaning of the body. The human body, with its sex - its masculinity and femininity - seen in the very mystery of creation, is not only a source of fruitfulness and of procreation, as in the whole natural order, but contains "from the beginning" the "spousal" attribute, that is, *the power to express love: precisely that love in which the human person becomes a gift* and – through this gift – fulfills the very meaning of his being and existence.[10]

---

[7] Gen. 2:23.
[8] Gen. 4:4.
[9] Cf. Gen. 14:18-20.
[10] Paul, John II. *Man and Woman He Created Them. A Theology of the Body.* Pauline Books and Media. Boston. 2006. 185-186.

It is true, everything thing about man's body and his masculinity is an offering; in that it protrudes to give. In contrast, everything about woman's body and her femininity is receptive; in that, it is open to being an offering. His and her bodies are complementary to each other by nature, which enables the mutual offering of spouses to participate in the Divine work of creation and bring forth the body, blood, and soul of new life on Earth. Similarly, in a work belonging to his own spousal order with Mother Church, the Priest consecrates the gifts of bread and wine brought to him that will become the Body, Blood, Soul, and Divinity of Jesus Christ. Indeed, the human bodies and the spousal union are *todah* and point to the Eucharist.

Even nature itself points to the Eucharist. From the motions of the stars and the planets, to the rays of our own sun and reflective light of the moon, to subatomic space particles, to rain, to seasonal patterns, to the lifecycle of plants and animals, all the universe seems created to do is to freely give itself away, just as its Creator gives His love away. In contrast, humans have proven to be the only living creatures who are inclined to think that they were created to take, rather than to offer. In fact, the greatest tragedy in the universe occurs whenever that attitude of being a taker, rather than being an offering, enters any of the Sacraments of the Church. Whether it be Holy Matrimony, Holy Orders, Holy Eucharist, or any of the other four sacraments, not disposing oneself to be an offering unto the Lord in the reception of the graces flowing out from the Sacraments is to approach God as a mercenary intending to kill the Spirit that lives within.

Along with prayer, confession, silently listening for God, and bodily worship, making a sacrificial offering to God, is just another one those acts belonging to our human nature that has reached its perfect expression in the Divine Symphony.

"The offerings are then brought forward. It is a praiseworthy practice for the bread and wine to be presented by the faithful."[11] Saint Justin Martyr attests to this tradition of the faithful expressing their participation in the sacrifice by making an offering of bread and wine,[12] but prior to finding its fulfillment in the Mass, a lesser ritual of the communion sacrifice can be found in Temple liturgical worship. The rubrics for the 'Communion Sacrifice Rite' of the Israelites is very similar to the rubrics in all the Catholic liturgies. Even the splashing of the blood of the lamb on the bread offering is fulfilled in the Mass with 'intinction,' 'consignation, and 'comixture.'

> This is the ritual for the communion sacrifice that is offered to the LORD. If someone offers it for thanksgiving, that person shall offer it with unleavened cakes mixed with oil, unleavened wafers spread with oil, and cakes made of bran flour mixed with oil and well kneaded. One shall present this offering together with loaves of leavened bread along with the thanksgiving communion sacrifice. From this the individual shall offer one bread of each type of offering as a contribution to the LORD; this shall belong to the priest who splashes the blood of the communion offering.[13]

One of my fondest memories of my time in discernment about joining the Melkite Greek-Catholic Church was the opportunity, Father Ignatius Harrington, pastor of Holy Resurrection Church in Columbus, Ohio, afforded me the opportunity to observe him perform the 'Liturgy of Preparation.' In the Divine Liturgy, since the sixth-century, the 'Liturgy of Preparation' has been a service set apart from the 'Liturgy of the Eucharist'; taking place prior to 'the Blessing of Incense and Veiling of the Gifts.'

---

[11] *GIRM*, III, 73.
[12] Cf. St. Justin, *Apol.* 1, 67.
[13] Lev. 7:11-14.

Originally it constituted a part of the Liturgy when the Deacon exclaimed: "Let us attend, that we may offer the Holy Oblation in peace," and where the prayer of the Oblation continues "to enable us to offer Thee Gifts." In the Liturgy of St. James, the prayer of the Preparation is read during the Liturgy. In the Liturgy of Clement, the prayer of Preparation took place after the dismissal of the Catechumens. St. Athanasios found untimely the practice of the preparation before the Divine Liturgy. St. Chrysostom put the Oblation and its prayer in the Liturgy after the kiss of peace and the exhortation, "Let us love one another," probably to remind us of the Bible's determination that "if thou bring thy gift to the altar and there rememberest that thy brother hath ought against thee, leave there thy gift before the altar and go thy way; first be reconciled to thy brother, then come and offer thy gift".[14]

Later in the 6th century, the office of the Preparation was set apart, elaborated, and officiated before the Divine Liturgy, as it is now. At the same time, the Cherubic hymn was inserted into the Liturgy against the protest of Patriarch Eutyhios (582). Symbolism and allegory entered this office of Preparation and somehow confused the coherence of the thoughts of the Liturgy by prescribing them in anticipation. The office of Preparation took its final shape in the 14th century.[15]

After the 'Prayers Before the Holy Doors', 'Entrance into the Altar', 'Vesting of the Deacon', 'Vesting of the Priest', and 'Washing of Hands', the Priest and Deacon offer a very ritualistic and meaningful preparation and blessing of the bread and wine that will become the Body and Blood of our Lord Jesus Christ. The bread called a 'posphoron' is a round loaf of leavened bread made from only flour, yeast, salt, and water. Any member of the

---

[14] Matt. 5: 23-24.
[15] *Introduction to the Divine Liturgy*. Greek Orthodox Archdiocese of America. (https://www.goarch.org/-/introduction-to-the-divine-liturgy). Retrieved 1/15/2018.

Church in good standing and whose conscience is clean may bake the 'posphoron' that is impressed in the center with the Greek letter stamp "IC-XC, NI-KA," abbreviations for Jesus Christ Conquers. The stamped cube in the center of posphoron is separated from the rest of the loaf and is placed on the holy Discos (paten). Later it will be consecrated and become the Lamb of God. The outside portions of the loaf are blessed prosphoras for the Saints, the Virgin Mary, and the living faithful and the faithfully departed. These incisions made into the 'posphoron' by the Priest's spear symbolically represents the pierce made into the Savior's side by the soldier's spear.[16] There on the Preparation Table, the holy Discos and Chalice remain until after the Cherubic Hymn when the Priest and Deacon process them to the Holy Table for the 'Prayers of Sanctification.'

> The Prothesis signifies the place of Calvary, where Jesus was "offered up" to God. Calvary was prefigured in the Old Testament by Abraham when God commanded him to make an altar of stone on a mountain, collect wood, and sacrifice his son on it. In his mercy, though, God allowed a ram to be offered instead. This was to show that the Father was pleased to allow, in "the fullness of time,"[17] His eternal Son to be incarnate of the pure virgin Theotokos and to be sacrificed for our sins. Though in His divinity He remained impassible (not subject to pain), nevertheless, as a man Christ suffered all His torments to the fullest -- and gladly because of His immense love for us.
>
> The Discos on which the bread is placed, according to the eighth century Patriarch of Constantinople, Saint Germanus, "represents the hands of Joseph of Arimathea and Nicodemus, who buried Christ. The Discos on which Christ is carried is also interpreted as the sphere of Heaven, manifesting to us in miniature the spiritual sun, Christ, and

---

[16] Cf. Jn. 19:34-35.
[17] Cf. Gal. 4:4; Eph. 1:10.

containing Him visibly in the bread. The Chalice corresponds to the vessel which received the mixture [of water and blood] which poured from the bloodied, undefiled side and from the hands and feet of Christ. Or again, the Chalice corresponds to the bowl which the Lord depicts, that is, Wisdom; because the Son of God has mixed His blood for drinking instead of wine, and set forth on His holy table, saying to all: Drink of my blood mixed for you for the remission of sins and eternal life.'"[18]

The cover on the Discos represents the cloth which covered Christ's face in the tomb. The veil, or the aer, is a rectangular ornamented veil for covering both the Chalice and Discos after the Proskomide. The aer corresponds to the stone which Joseph placed over the entrance of the tomb and which Pilate's guards then sealed. It can also represent the shroud which contained the Lord's body.[19]

While the liturgies of the Latin Church may not be as ritualistic as those in the East, the intention and the symbolism is the same. Not even every Eastern liturgy is equal in subjective beauty. For example, the 'Preparation of the Offerings' of the Antiochian Catholic Church is very brief. Indeed, the many liturgies of the Universal Church are not equally rich or equally mysterious to each other, but they are all the same in substance. For, there is only one Divine Symphony that we call the *Ite, Missa est*. There is not a different Real Presence of Jesus at the Novus Ordo than there is at the Liturgy of Saint John Chrysostom. To teach such would be a heresy. On the contrary, there is only one Divine Symphony, but various compositions of that singular Divine reality.

---

[18] Germans of Constantinople, *On the Divine Liturgy*, 38-39.
[19] Najim, Michael and Frazier, T. L. *Understanding the Orthodox Liturgy: A Guide for Participating in the Liturgy of St. John Chrysostom*. 26.

Returning to the Tridentine and Novus Ordo rites; while Order of the Mass states that "other gifts to relieve the needs of the Church and of the poor" may be offered during this subject of the liturgy, the bread and wine are the primary and only required offerings, because they are the only offerings that can become the Body, Blood, Soul, and Divinity of Jesus Christ. While a flock of chickens, oil, flax, or monetary offering, or a new golden chalice and paten may be our acceptable sacrifice and contribute to the needs of the Church, these sacrificial offerings cannot directly aid us in our journey to eternal life, precisely because they are never transubstantiated; they never become another substance; they never become the Real Presence of Jesus Christ Himself for our consumption and salvation.

THE PRAYER OVER THE OFFERINGS

The Priest, now standing at the altar, takes the paten with the bread and holds it slightly raised above the altar with both hands, saying in a low voice, or saying aloud if there is not an Offertory Chant, "**Blessed are you, Lord God of all creation, for through your goodness we have received the bread we offer you: fruit of the earth and work of human hands, it will become for us the bread of life.**" Then after he then places the paten with the bread on the corporal, he or the Deacon pours wine and a little water into the chalice, saying quietly, or saying aloud if there is not an Offertory Chant, "**By the mystery of this water and wine may we come to share in the divinity of Christ who humbled himself to share in our humanity.**"

The Priest then takes the chalice with both hands and holds it slightly raised above the altar and in a low voice says, "**Blessed are you, Lord God of all creation, for through your goodness we have received the wine we offer you: fruit of the vine and work of human hands, it will become our spiritual drink.**" After this confessional prayer, he then places the chalice on the corporal.

To both confessional prayers, the People of God acclaim, **"Blessed be God forever,"** unless there is an Offertory Chant being presented.

The mystery of water and wine being mixed has to immediately be connected to the *Gospel of John's* account of one of the soldiers at Jesus' crucifixion piercing Him on the side with a spear, and "at once there came out blood and water. He who saw it has borne witness – his testimony is true, and he knows that he tells the truth – that you also may believe."[20]

Secondarily, it also has to be connected to Jesus' miracle at the Wedding Feast in Cana where water was turned into wine, which was a sign of the tran-substantive nature of the Presence of Christ in our life that brings about our salvation and divinization. Not only the Sacrament of the Holy Eucharist, the blood and water pouring out of Jesus' side also point to effects of Baptism and all of the sacraments, and even to the Church Herself. In one of his homilies on *John*, Saint Augustine of Hippo has this to say:

> Here was opened wide the door of life, from which the sacraments of the Church have flowed out, without which there is no entering in unto the life which is true life. [...] Here the second Adam with bowed head slept upon the cross, that thence a wife might be formed of him, flowing from His side while He slept. O, death, by which the dead come back to life! Is there anything purer than this blood, any wound more healing!

The first thing that the author of *John* wants us to know about Jesus' miracle at Wedding Feast in Cana is that it took place "on the third day."[21] To understand what *John* means by the "third day" we must revisit his earlier chapters to discover his

---

[20] Jn. 19:34-35.
[21] Jn. 2:1.

theological chronology. By the time he gets to the Wedding Feast the author has already written about four days of the new creation (sequenced by the opening phrase, "On the next day..."), so when we see that the Wedding Feast took place on the "third day", what he is conveying is that this is the third day after the fourth day, which makes it day seven (the Sabbath), according to his theological chronology of the new creation. In this way, *John* is playing off of *Genesis*, where we read that "God blessed the seventh day and made it holy."[22]

It was a definitely an unfortunate event for the wedding festivities the run out of wine. Allegorically, the wedding became just like Cain and not able to bear fruit. Yet, what happened next was something very intimate. After being prompted by His Mother, the Lord told the servers to fill the jars with water. Inasmuch as Jesus was fully capable of doing this type of labor Himself, it was proper for the community to participate in their blessing. The virgin jars were filled to the brim with water; that is, the vessel and water, which had previously been separate and foreign to one another, had now become one, and out of this intimate and Divine union came Heavenly fruit.

Jesus, the new Adam, blessed the Wedding at Cana and gave us all a prototype sign of future blessings when He had water (a symbol of the Holy Spirit) poured into six pure (set apart) vessels, which represent man and woman who were created on the sixth day. Only after these pure vessels had been filled with water were they able to bring forth the fruit of the vine (wine/love/Blood of Christ). The meaning of the imagery here is that whenever man is filled with the Holy Spirit, he will produce fruit.

Together with the New Adam, the presence of the Virgin Mary, the New Eve, at the Wedding Feast in Cana also connects

---

[22] Gen. 2:3.

Interesting

the Eucharist and all the Sacraments to God's promise of new life through His Church.

When Mary comes to her Son and says to Him, "They have no wine," and He responds to her by saying, "Woman, how does your concern affect me? My hour has not yet come,"[23] the word "Woman" here is not an insult or something pejorative. On the contrary, what *John* is conveying here is that Jesus had just paid His mother the highest compliment. Again, we must understand *Genesis* if we are going to understand *John*. The first time the word 'woman' is used in the Bible was at the creation of 'woman.' In Hebrew, the word that Jesus would have used is 'isha' (alef shin hey – אישה) (pronounced ee-SHAH). Similarly, man or adam in Hebrew is simply 'ish.' Therefore, the first compliment Jesus gives His mother is by calling her 'isha.' In this way, He is raising Mary up to her true dignity of being the new Eve. He also compliments her in a second way when He calls her 'isha,' by acknowledging that she is part of, and comes from, and is for 'ish.' In other words, Jesus is acknowledging here that His mother Mary is truly wo-man – truly isha in that she is precisely to man – to ish what she was created to be for him.

Then when He asked, "how does your concern affect me?" the author of the *Gospel of John* means to demonstrate here how the new Eve is different from the first Eve. That is, while the first Eve pressed upon her husband a concern of hers that led to the fall of humanity, the New Eve presses upon her Son a concern of His that lead to the restoration of humanity.

Then the new Eve tells her Son what this concern has to do with Him when she tells the servers, "Do whatever he tells you."[24] Oh, how I wish we would all just listen to Mary today. Again, this is quite a contrast from the first woman who vacated

---

[23] Jn. 2:4.
[24] Jn. 2:5.

her position of being precisely what she was created to be for ish. While the first Eve told the ish who she had been created for to do what he should not have done, the new Eve trusts the ish who she had been created for to do what He was called to do, by telling the servers to "Do whatever He tells you."

Altogether the mystery of the water and wine informs us that the Sacrifice of the Mass is most like existence because it only exists to divinize us; that is, it exists only to configure us into the image of Christ Jesus. There is nothing else on Earth that does what the Mass promises to do. Knowing this one simple thing should be enough to convince any Catholic to never again causally approach, enter, or participate in the Divine Symphony, but, instead, be a child who is passionately purposed to pray and confess the Mass so that they might be made holy and be forever found in the Presence of God.

After the People have acclaimed, **"Blessed be God forever,"** or the Offertory Chant has been concluded, the Priest, bowing profoundly, quietly prays, **"With humble spirit and contrite heart may we be accepted by you, O Lord, and may our sacrifice in your sight this day be pleasing to you, Lord God."** This petition that God will *accept* us qualifies this prayer the third sacramental absolution (after the Penitential Rite). As compared to the Eastern rites, this is a meager number of sacramental absolutions, but nevertheless beautiful and significant in the manner in which this petition recapitulates David's Prayer of Repentance in *Psalm* 51, "For you do not desire sacrifice or I would give it; a burnt offering you would not accept. My sacrifice, O God, is a contrite spirit; a contrite, humble heart, O God, you will not scorn."

It is as valid then as it is in the liturgy today; the act of making an offering or performing a sacrifice that is disassociated from the type of deposition that allows us to receive Him worthily is not pleasing to God. Cain's lackadaisical sacrifice reflected a disposition that was disinterested in being loved by God.[25] Similarly, the offering of Ananias and Sapphira reflected that they were not disposed to giving everything they had to God.[26] They, like the rich young man,[27] were not yet ready to endure the temporary pain and misery that disassociating ourselves from worldly comforts pours upon the selfish nature. They were not yet ready to depend on God for everything.

On the contrary, it is only a humble and contrite spirit; a disposition that truly believes that all that I am and all that I have comes from God, and acts on that belief by offering all that I am and all that I have back to God. It is that type of trusting disposition that the Priest prays that God searches us for so that our sacrifice will be acceptable to Him. For this the Priest prays not just as David prayed, but also as Azariah prayed as he stood up in the midst of the fire:

> We have in our day no prince, prophet, or leader; no burnt offering, sacrifice, oblation, or incense, no place to offer first fruits, to find favor with you. But with contrite heart and humble spirit let us be received; As though it were burnt offerings of rams and bulls or tens of thousands of fat lands, so let our sacrifice be in our presence today and find favor before you; for those who trust in you cannot be put to shame.[28]

I have often been saddened by some Priests who appear to be tremendously casual in their intercessions for us. I have also been inspired with awe by the appearance of some whom I can tell are enduring great pains as they pray. It as if though they are weeping as Christ wept, and God's Presence of silence returns to primacy whenever these Priests kneel and intercede for us. There is always a danger of becoming lazy regarding things we

---

[25] Cf. Gen. 4:3.
[26] Cf. Acts. 5:1-11.
[27] Cf. Mt. 19:22.
[28] Dn. 3:15-17.

do with high degrees of repetition, and Priests are humans like the rest of us. They can and are allowed to become disinterested in things, but for that reason, I encourage you to always pray for the holiness of our Priests; that their will might always be strengthened through the Holy Spirit and Mary our Immaculate Mother.

After the Priest rises from praying, he may incense the offerings, the cross, and the altar, and, after which, a Deacon or other minister will then incense the Priest and the people; thereby, bringing life to the *Psalm* that is recited by the Priest in the High Mass of the Tridentine Rite, **"Welcome as incense-smoke let my prayer rise up before Thee, O Lord. When I lift up my hands, be it as acceptable as the evening sacrifice. O Lord, set a guard before my mouth, a barrier to fence in my lips. Do not turn my heart towards thoughts of evil, to make excuses for sins."**[29] Incensing the offerings of bread, wine, and the People is also a fulfillment of what our Lord Jesus showed John:

> Another angel came and stood at the altar, holding a gold censer. He was given a great quality of incense to offer, along with the prayers of all the holy ones, on the gold altar that was before the throne. The smoke of the incense along with the prayers of the holy ones went up before God from the hand of the angel.[30]

Having prayed for a pure heart, the Priest now stands at the side of the altar and performs the symbolic gesture of washing his hands to signify the purity and inner cleanliness required of those who stand in the Presence of God to offer sacrifice. In the Novus Ordo Rite, the Priest washes his hands and quietly says, **"Wash me, O Lord, from my iniquity and cleanse me from my sin."** Yet, this prayer is but an abbreviation of the *Psalm* that is recited

---

[29] Ps. 141:2-3.
[30] Rev. 8:3-4.

in the Tridentine Rite at this same moment, and in the Divine Liturgy of Saint John Chrysostom after the 'Vesting' ceremonies:

> **I will wash my hands in innocence so that I may process around your altar, Lord, to hear the sound of thanksgiving, and recount all your wondrous deeds. Lord, I love the refuge of your house, the site of the dwelling-place of your glory. Do not take me away with sinners, nor my life with the men of blood, in whose hands there is a plot, their right hands full of bribery. But I walk in my integrity; redeem me, be gracious to me! My foot stands on level ground; in assemblies I will bless the LORD.**[31]

If you follow *Exodus* from chapters 27 through 30, you will notice how closely it mirrors the opening rites of the Liturgy of Saint John Chrysostom. From the arrangement of the Tabernacle to the 'Vesting of the Priest and Deacon,' to the 'Consecration of the Priests', to the 'Incensing,' there is an unambiguous fulfillment of Old Covenant liturgy in the Catholic Mass. Of course, the same elements and fulfillment are present in the liturgies of the West, but not as linear and not as unclouded.

Nevertheless, what is intended to be taken from these rituals in the Latin liturgies is the recognition, comprehension, and internalization of the allegory found in the progression and transformation of activity, which is evident by a number of new subjects. For example, there had been an incensing of the altar and the people, so that their prayers might reach the Heavens. The Priest had moved to the side of the altar and entered into a ritual of purification, just as Priest of the Covenant had always done prior to entering into the Tabernacle or Holy of Holies. Also, up until this moment, the People of God's only audible participation in the Liturgy of the Eucharist was in affirming the

---

[31] Ps. 26:6-12.

blessing of their sacrifices by acclaiming in a double periodic phrasing, "**Blessed be God for ever.**"

Now, the Priest stands facing the People (if not ad orientem) at the middle of the altar, where he extends and then joins his hands together, and says, "**Pray, brethren (brothers and sisters), that my sacrifice and yours may be acceptable to God, the almighty Father.**" To which the People of God rise and reply, "**May the Lord accept the sacrifice at your hands for the praise and glory of His name, for our good and the good of all His holy Church.**" Heretofore, the People of God's only intercession for their Priest had been in response to his audible intercessions for them, to which they replied, "**And with your spirit.**" Yet, now, in response to his prayer that God will find their sacrifice worthy, the People desperately intercede for their Priest; that through his purified hands their sacrifice, which will become the Body, Blood, Soul, and Divinity of Jesus Christ, will be not just for the benefit of their salvation, but also for the salvation of His Universal Church.

Then the Priest, standing in the orans posture (arms outstretched), says the Prayer over the Offerings, of which there are many for the Priest to choose from. At the end of that prayer, the People of God acclaim, "**Amen.**"

To complete 'the Offertory' and introduce the oblation of the Sacrifices in Eucharistic Prayers, in the Tridentine Rite, the Priest silently (in secret) offers another prayer of intercession for God's People, "**Sanctify, we beseech Thee, O Lord our God, by the invocation of Thy holy Name, the Sacrifice we offer, and through its means make us ourselves a perfect offering forever. Through our Lord Jesus Christ Thy Son, Who liveth and reigneth with Thee in the unity of the Holy Ghost, God.**" He then says loud enough for the server to hear, "**World without end,**" and the server responds, "**Amen.**"

In the Missa Cantata (Lat. for "sung Mass") liturgy according to the Dominican Rite, the Priest intercedes secretly in silence, **"May this offering, O Lord, we beseech You, wipe away our transgressions, and make holy the mind and bodies of Your servants for celebrating this sacrifice."** Then aloud he says, **"Through Jesus Christ, thy Son for Lord, Who liveth and reigneth with thee, in the unity of the Holy Ghost, ever one God, world without end."** To which the People respond, **"Amen."**

With this, the first section of the third movement of the Divine Symphony has concluded, and will now transition into the second section of Eucharistic Prayers. Whereas, in the classical symphony the second section of the minuet consists of a smaller group of instruments, so too is the central subject matter of our prayers and confessions to God narrowed down to the Passover memorial and sacrifice.

The New Covenant Seder Liturgy

To understand the 'the Eucharistic Prayers,' it is helpful first to understand what Scripture, Tradition, and history have revealed about the character and purpose of the Passover sacrifice and the liturgy associated with it.

The vital character mark of the Passover feast is that it has always been a Divinely commanded life-giving sacrifice. Christ Jesus fulfilled the original command[32] to perpetually sacrifice the Passover lamb in Himself through the Liturgy of Holy Eucharist. That this sacrifice feast affords us eternal life is what makes it also an opportunity for celebration.

The purpose of Christ Jesus' Passover feast with His disciples, commonly called the Last Supper, but more appropriately called the First Supper or the First New Covenant Seder, is to gather those *In* Christ to renew their covenant vows with Him by

---

[32] Cf. Exo. 12:14.

drinking His Blood and celebrating their betrothal to the Bridegroom by taking His Body into theirs. In this way, the Sacrament of the Liturgy of the Holy Eucharist is the fulfillment of Jewish Seder liturgy, and the First New Covenant Seder was just the first of many to come in which Christ Jesus would give Himself to us entirely through His Real Presence in the transubstantiated[33] Bread and Wine.

The various eyewitness accounts of the Passover feast helps us greatly in unfolding its character marks. The Passover feast in *Matthew* and *Mark* concludes with the same prophetic saying from Jesus that *Luke's* account opens with, "I have eagerly desired to eat this Passover with you before I suffer, for, I tell you, I shall not eat it [again] until there is fulfillment in the Kingdom of God."[34] In fact, *Luke* has Jesus repeating His prophecy a second time as He partakes of the second of four traditional cups of wine served at the Jewish Passover feast. "Then He took a cup, gave thanks, and said, "Take this and share it among yourselves; for I tell you [that] from this time on I shall not drink of the fruit of the vine until the Kingdom of God comes."[35]

---

[33] *Transubstantiation* is the scholastic term used to designate the unique change in the Holy Eucharistic bread and wine into the Body and Blood of Christ Jesus. *Transubstantiation* indicates that through/after the consecration/confection of the bread and the wine by the Priest at Mass, a change occurs in which the entire substance of the bread becomes the substance of the Body of Christ and the entire substance of the wine becomes the Blood of Christ - even though the appearance or 'species' of bread and wine remain (Cf. CCC 1376). In other words, the *substance* (the essence; gist; matter) of the bread and wine is changed into the *substance* of the Christ. What is not changed is that which is not a part of the *substance*; that is, the color, shape, appearance, smell, taste, and etcetera. Through consecration (Christ Jesus working through His Priest), the *substance* is transferred but not exchanged, meaning the bread and wine truly becomes the Body and Blood of Jesus Christ, and what was formerly the substance of the bread and wine is no more. *Transubstantiation* is a miracle, brought about by the loving and creative power of the Divine Word.

[34] Lk. 22:15-16.

[35] Lk. 22:17-18.

Although Christ Jesus' command, "Do this in memory of Me" is only recorded in *Luke*, these remain to be six of the most powerful words in all of sacred Scripture, because they have profound and eternal implications for all of humanity! For, if Christ did indeed meet the conditions of the Old Covenant Seder, then, consequently, it means that with these six words He also fulfilled and propelled it (i.e., the Seder Passover liturgy) into the New Covenant in the form of a command, "Do this in memory of Me."

The Greek word for *memory* here is *anemeno*, which is a compound word derived from the prefix *ana* (meaning: repetition, intensity, reversal) and *meno* (meaning: continue, tarry, stand, expectancy), together they combine to mean *perpetually wait*. It is important to note that this command of Jesus is perfectly fulfilled in the *anamnesis* subject of 'the Eucharistic Prayers.' While *anemeno* is not used anywhere else in sacred Scripture, Saint Paul frequently referred to this same theme of 'waiting' through use of the word *Parousia*, which is the coming/the Presence of the Lord.[36] In addition, the letters attributed to Ss. James, Peter, and John also admonish their readers to wait in perseverance for the Parousia patiently.[37]

Throughout sacred Scripture we can clearly and consistently witness Christ Jesus working within the written and oral laws, not to destroy, but rather to fulfill them.[38] It then follows, therefore, that if the Catholic Sacrament of the Eucharist is indeed the fulfilled Seder, then we should be able to point to Scripture and Tradition to demonstrate how Christ both met the requirements of the Old Law and brought it to true bloom in its fulfilled meaning.

The examination as to whether the Passover Feast of Unleavened Bread, which Jesus shared with His disciples, met the

---

[36] Cf. 1 Cor. 15:23; 1 Thess. 2:19, 3:13, 4:15, 5:23; 2 Thess. 2:1,8,9.
[37] Cf. Jas. 5:7,8; 2 Pet. 1:16, 3:4,12; 1 Jn. 2:28.
[38] Cf. Mt. 5:17.

three requirements of having been a genuine Seder begins by examining the first condition, which concerns whether the instant Feast took place on the fourteenth day of Nisan.[39] The orthodox Jewish response is that if the Seder did not take place on the prescribed day reserved for it, then it was not valid. Fortunately, the Gospel of Mark clearly states that "On the first day of the Feast of Unleavened Bread, when they sacrificed the Passover lamb, His disciples said to Him, "Where do you want us to go and prepare for you to eat the Passover?"[40]

The second requirement, which was also met by Jesus and His disciples, was that the Passover could only be celebrated in Jerusalem.[41] Continuing in the Marcan account, "He sent two of His disciples and said to them, "Go into the city and a man will meet you, carrying a jar of water. Follow him. Wherever he enters, say to the master of the house, 'The Teacher says, "Where is my guest room where I may eat the Passover with my disciples?" Then he will show you a large upper room furnished and ready. Make the preparations for us there." The disciples then went off, entered the city, and found it just as he had told them; and they prepared the Passover."[42] There is every indication in sacred Scripture that the 'city' being referred to here is the city of Jerusalem.

Now we turn to the third requirement; the actual Passover feast liturgy. According to Jewish tradition, there are four cups of wine that are poured and drunk during Seder,[43] with the first cup being mixed (wine cut with water) during the *Kiddush*, in which various traditional prayers and sanctifying events take place. The Synoptic Gospels do not tell us whether any elements

---

[39] Cf. Exo. 12:6; Dt. 16:1-6; Num. 28:16-17.

[40] Mk. 14:12; Cf. Mt. 26:17-19; Lk. 22:7-13.

[41] Cf. Dt. 16:5-6; Mt. 26:18.

[42] Mk. 14:12-16; Cf. Mt. 26:17-19; Lk. 22:7-13.

[43] Each cup represents one of the four promises that YHWH made to the Israelites while they were still being held captive in Egypt (Cf. Exo. 6:6).

of the *Kiddush* had taken place, but because the Gospels do not indicate that any prayers were offered before they began eating, it would not be unreasonable for us to believe that these thirteen Jewish men did offer some form of thanksgiving praise to God before they ate. That is, the absence of the *Kiddush* in Scripture does not mean that it did not take place, but rather because it was such a standard element in all Jewish liturgy, it leads us to believe that it did take place, especially if we can point to evidence of a significant number of other elements of the Seder as being present at this feast.

After the *Kiddush*, they would have eaten lettuce dipped in salt water or vinegar, vegetables together with the cake of *matzah*, and two cooked things. Afterward, the second Seder cup would have been mixed.

The next portion of Seder is even more liturgical in nature, in that the head of the family takes time to recount the story of the exodus. A clear image of the Old Covenant Seder liturgy is recorded in the <u>Mishnah</u>:

> The second cup is mixed. The son asks his father the four questions, and if the son does not have enough knowledge his father teaches him how to ask: "Why is this night different from all other nights? On the other nights, we eat leavened or unleavened bread, but this night only unleavened. On all other nights, we eat a variety of vegetables, but on this night only bitter herbs. On all other nights, we may eat meat which has been roasted, stewed, or boiled, but this night only roast meat. On all other nights, we dip our food only once, but on this night twice." The father then instructs him according to his son's level of knowledge. He begins with the disgrace and ends with the glory [[story from the *Haggadah*]], and he expounds from "A wandering Aramean was my father..." (Deuteronomy 26:5), until he finished the whole story.[44]

---

[44] *Pesahim* 10:4.

Rabban Gamaliel used to say: Whoever has not spoken of these three things at Passover has not fulfilled his obligations: *Pesah*,[45] *Matzah*,[46] and *Maror*.[47] *Pesah*, because God passed over the houses of our fathers in Egypt. *Matzah*, because our fathers were redeemed out of Egypt. *Maror*, because the Egyptians made the lives of our fathers bitter in Egypt. In each and every generation, a man must think of himself as if he came out of Egypt, as it is written: "And you shall tell your son on that day saying, it is because of that which the Lord did for me when I came forth out of Egypt" (Exodus 13:8). Therefore, we are required to give thanks, to praise, to glorify, to honor, to exalt, to extol, and to bless Him who performed all those wonders for our fathers and for us. He brought us from bondage to freedom, from sorrow to gladness, from mourning to Festival, from darkness to great light, and from slavery to redemption. Let us say before Him: Hallelujah.[48]

Likewise, in the Scriptures we witness Jesus giving an actual and liturgical fulfillment of this tradition when He foretells the New Covenant exodus. When Jesus took His place among the Apostles and said to them, "I have eagerly desired to eat this Passover with you before I suffer, for, I tell you, I shall not eat it [again] until its fulfillment in the Kingdom of God," He instantly met and fulfilled the prescribed ritual of the Seder by telling His Apostles how this night is different from every other night. That is, He points to Himself as being the new *Pesah* that will suffer and die for the sins of many. Later during the feast, He will also point to Himself as being the new and true *Matzah* (manna) that gives eternal life, and as the new *Maror* whom the world will make

---

[45] Pesah is the lamb or kid slaughtered and eaten in ancient times on the first evening of Passover.

[46] Matzah is the unleavened bread, required in ancient times in connection with all sacrifices in the Temple in Jerusalem, and in all Jewish homes during the seven (later eight) days of Passover.

[47] Maror is the bitter herbs eaten at the Passover Seder.

[48] *Pesahim* 10:5.

things bitter for, and bitter for those who are members of His body.[49]

The fulfillment of what Rabbi Gamaliel said is true. In the New Covenant Seder, we are commanded by Christ Jesus Himself to give thanks, to praise, to glorify, to honor, to exalt, to extol, and to bless Him who performed all those wonders for our fathers and for us. We offer precisely these things at the Catholic Mass every day when we offer the sacrifice in *anemeno* of our Risen Lord. What Rabbi Gamaliel did not know is that Christ Jesus is the one who brought us out of bondage to true freedom, from sorrow to true gladness, from mourning to true festival, from darkness to true light, and from slavery to true redemption. Indeed, before our Lord Jesus, we always say Hallelujah.

Moreover, there are three senses of food that this command brings to perfection in the Holy Eucharist. In the first sense, the 'this' that Christ Jesus is referring to in this command is the New Covenant Passover (Eucharist), which is food for the salvation of our soul. Whereas, before we celebrated the Passover Feast of Unleavened Bread in memory of God's delivery of us out of physical bondage from the Egyptians, we now do it in memory of our true delivery out of the spiritual bondage (sin and death) through His death on the Cross. To paraphrase Jesus here, 'Now celebrate the Passover in memory of Me,' or 'Now celebrate the Passover in memory of My redemption of you from your true enemy.'

In the second sense of this command, the 'this' that Jesus is referring to in this command is the New Manna, which is food for the body (Corporeal and Spiritual). From the very beginning of His life, here on Earth, Jesus was understood to be food. As an infant, He was laid in a feeding trough (manger), which was used

---

[49] Cf. Exo. 12:8-9.

to feed the other animals who were created on the sixth day.[50] The Hebrew word for living body is *basar*, which means 'the total self, the flesh, and the full essence of man.' Therefore, when Christ Jesus commands us to "Do this in *anemeno* of Me," He is not just referring to celebrating the new Passover Seder, but is also instructing us in how to live, how to love, and how to follow Him. To paraphrase, 'You also give your total self over for those whom you love in *anemeno* of Me giving myself over for you.' This language of sacrificial love embedded in the Eucharist is echoed in the command, "Love one another as I loved you. No one has greater love than this, to lay down one's life [one's total self] for one's friends."[51] Every time we receive the Holy Eucharist we are confessing our love for God, neighbor, and self and with that confession follows the responsibility to live it out.

In a third sense, the 'this' that Jesus is referring to in His command is the sacred Scripture, which is food for the mind. It is tied to the Mosaic command to "Therefore, take these words of mine into your heart and soul. Bind them at your wrist as a sign, and let them be a pendant on your forehead."[52] It was clear to the Jews that God's words were a means to achieve eternal life. The *tefillin*, which is composed of two sets of leather boxes (containing four passages from the Torah - two from *Exodus* and two from *Deuteronomy*), is tied to the head and arm by means of leather straps, helping the Jew to focus within by the restraints imposed from without; thereby enabling a humble and uninterrupted contemplation of God's commandments and placing the adherent in a state of constant awareness of God's Presence. Because of the materials that form the *tefillin* (i.e., leather, parchment wrapped in calf's tail hair) are edible, devotees believed that the word of God was symbolically comestible. Through the New Covenant

---

[50] Cf. Lk. 2:7.
[51] Jn. 15:12-13.
[52] Dt. 11:18; Cf. Exo. 13:9,12; Dt. 6:8.

Seder, Christ Jesus fulfills this Mosaic command to wear the *te-fillin*. That is, the Word of God is no longer thought as something that could be eaten but actually is eaten. The Word of God is no longer worn on outside of our body, but is truly taken into us; meaning that we are no longer conformed from the outside in, but now from the inside out.

Now, turning back to the Seder, after Jesus told His Apostles about the new exodus, they would have drunken the second cup of wine and entered into the third section of the Seder, which is the actual feast, commencing with 'the Breaking of Bread.' We can see this portion of the Seder clearly in all of the Synoptic Gospels where Jesus took the bread, said the blessing, broke it, and gave it to them saying, "This is my body, which will be given for you; do this in *anemeno* of Me."

According to the *Mishnah*, after the feast, the third cup would have been mixed and blessed:

> After the third cup has been mixed, the leader says the blessings after the feast. Before the fourth cup, he completes the *Hallel* and then says the blessing over the song. If he wishes to drink wine between the cups, he may do so. But he may not drink between the third and fourth cups.[53]

Again, sacred Scripture confirms that this requirement of the Seder took place on the night before Jesus was crucified, in saying, "And likewise the cup after they had eaten, saying, "This cup is the new covenant in my Blood, which will be shed for you." God's promissory Covenants are always sealed and renewed with blood, by which they also become familial bonds, as we see here with God and man sharing the same blood. Therefore, by fulfilling the meaning of the cups of wine, from this point forward, there would no longer be four cups containing merely the fruit of

---

[53] *Pesahim* 10:7.

the vine, but one cup of His Life, of His Love, of His Truth, and of His Death.

Whereas in the Old Covenant, Moses took the blood of the lamb, "sprinkled it on the people, saying, "This is the blood of the covenant which YHWH has made with you in accordance with all these words of His,"[54] Christ Jesus, the true Lamb of YHWH, told His disciples to drink His Blood and said, "this is my Blood of the Covenant, which will be shed on behalf of many for the forgiveness of sins." Whereas the blood of the first lamb, repeatedly sacrificed, bound the Israelites to the law and atoned for their sins, the Blood of the second Lamb, sacrificed once and for all, binds us to the Holy Spirit and brought Salvation from sin.[55]

Concerning the fourth cup, *Matthew* informs us that after they had eaten the Passover feast, they sang a hymn and "went out to the Mount of Olives."[56] We know from the *Mishnah* (as cited above) that the third cup of wine was drunk immediately after the feast. Therefore, being that so many requirements of the Seder had already been met, there is no reason to believe that the fourth cup was not drunk after the *Hallel* (traditionally *Psalms* 112 through 118) was sung and the final blessing was given.[57]

The popular counter-position posits Jesus did not drink the fourth cup. The basis for this claim relies on three Scriptural proofs: 1) In *Matthew* and *Mark*, after Jesus pours the cup of His blood of the covenant, He states that he will not drink the fruit of the vine again until He drinks it in the Kingdom of God;[58] 2) Also in *Matthew's* and *Mark's* accounts, there is no mention of a cup

---

[54] Exo. 24:8.
[55] Cf. Heb. 9-10.
[56] Mt. 26:30.
[57] *Psalm* 114 recounts the theme of the entire Passover ritual.
[58] Cf. Mt. 26:27-30; Mk. 14:24-26.

that was drunk after the Passover meal; and 3) In all three Synoptic Gospels, Jesus is recorded asking His Father to let pass/remove *this cup* from Him, if it be His will.[59]

There are five problems with this counter-position. In summary; first, *Luke* attests to Jesus stating first that He will not eat the Passover meal again "until there is fulfillment in the Kingdom of God," and then that He will not "drink of the fruit of the vine until the Kingdom of God comes." Therefore, if we are going to argue because *Matthew* and *Mark* reads that Jesus would not drink from the vine again, it then, therefore, implies that Jesus did not drink the fourth cup, then it must then, therefore, follow that *Luke's* claim about Jesus not eating the Passover meal again, also implies that He did not eat any of the meal (including the bread or lamb) either.

Second, there is a problem with suggesting that 'not again' is inclusive of that particular Passover meal. Rather, it would be more consistent with Scripture to take Jesus statement here as being a prophecy of His death; that He was prophesying that He would not be around for next year's Passover meal, but would only partake of this meal again after His death and resurrection. To find the fulfillment of Jesus' profound and prophetic statement all we need to do to find out where the Kingdom is at now, and then we will discover where Jesus fulfilled this prophetic statement and broke bread with His disciples again (i.e., after this prophetic statement of His). Fortunately for us, to find such an occurrence, we need not look very far at all, "And it happened that, while He was with them at table, He took bread, said the blessing, broke it, and gave it to them."[60] There it was, after His resurrection, when the fulfillment of 'the Kingdom of God' came

---

[59] Cf. Mt. 26:39; Mk. 14:36; Lk. 26:42.
[60] Lk. 24:30.

with Jesus and His Apostles sharing the New Covenant Seder (Holy Eucharist) again.

Third, those who make this argument of the fourth cup of Passover not being drunken, cherry-pick *Matthew* and *Mark* so that *Luke* can be excluded. They would rather do that, than to reconcile the fact that not only does *Luke* mention that there was a cup drunken after the Passover meal, but according to the Seder Ritual, it was *Luke's* fourth cup that was the Blood of Covenant, rather than *Matthew* and *Mark* in which it was the third cup that was the Blood of the Covenant. If the cup referred to here by Jesus in the Garden of Agony is to be taken literally and attached to the Passover meal ritual, then for *Luke* that would be the fifth cup. Moreover, just because *Luke* does not mention that a song was sung after the Passover meal, does not mean that they did not sing the *Hallel*.

Fourth, those who argue that Jesus did not drink the fourth cup illogically make an argument from silence that can be applied to the whole Passover meal. Through a myopic and Protestant-like sola-scriptura reading of *Matthew* and *Mark*, they argue that Jesus did not complete the Seder ritual, because those two Gospels do not mention Jesus drinking from the fourth cup. The Scriptures also do not say that whether there was an actual lamb at the meal, or if that lamb had been sacrificed by the High Priest. There is no mention of the five types of bitter herbs. Nor do the Scriptures mention whether the *Kiddush* had taken place or not. There is mention of preparations being made in an upper room in the city,[61] but had everything leavened been burned in that house prior to the meal? Due to none of these things being mentioned, are we to believe that Jesus was suddenly disobedient to what He had practiced all His life?

---

[61] Cf. Lk. 22:10-13.

Finally, Jesus was a faithful Jew who used His finally Passover meal ritual to fulfill it and bring it into the New Covenant as a command to it in *anemeno* of Him. To suggest that Jesus did not fulfill the Passover ritual has grave Christological implications, and to do so based primarily on sola-scriptura and arguments from silence, is entirely errant from the Catholic senses of understanding sacred Scripture. On the contrary, because we can read so many other elements of the Passover Seder ritual present in the texts, it is, therefore, logical to conclude that Christ Jesus was faithful to them all.

Now, as we move back into discussing 'the Eucharistic Prayers,' there are three summary points of the Old Covenant Passover sacrifice feast being fulfilled by Christ Jesus in the sacrament of the Holy Eucharist that should be taken with us:

1. Whereas, in the Old Covenant, soon before the Israelites were delivered from slavery in Egypt, God commanded them to do this (the Passover sacrifice and feast) forever in memory of when the Lord spared the Israelites by passing over their houses, but struck down the Egyptians,[62] now in the New Covenant, soon before those who were in the bondage to sin and death were delivered from it, by the way of the Cross, they were commanded by Christ to "Do this in *anemeno* of Me." God commanded His people to offer this memorial sacrifice and feast forever,[63] and it has never ceased in the Catholic Church.

2. Whereas in the Old Covenant, the roasted flesh of the lamb was eaten with unleavened bread,[64] now, the New Covenant, we are commanded to eat the Flesh of Christ Jesus under the guise of unleavened bread. "Then He

---

[62] Cf. Exo. 12:27.
[63] Cf. Exo. 12:14.
[64] Cf. Exo. 12:8.

took the bread, said the blessing, broke it, and gave it to them, saying, "This is my body, which will be given for you; do this in *anemeno* of Me."

3. Whereas, in the Old Covenant, God commanded the Israelites to apply the blood of the lamb to the two doorposts and lintel of every house in which they partook of the lamb,[65] so that they would be passed-over, now, in the New Covenant, we are commanded to drink the Blood of the true lamb under the guise of wine; taking it into ourselves, so that we will be passed-over (have eternal life). "And likewise, the cup after they had eaten, saying, "This cup is the New Covenant in my Blood, which will be shed for you." [66]

THE PREFACE DIALOGUE

The *Sursum corda* (Lat. for "lift up your hearts" or literally, "Hearts lifted") is one of the oldest periodic phrasings in Divine Symphony, and it remains today as the preface of 'the Eucharistic Prayers' preceding 'the Sanctus' in every Catholic liturgy, and even those of the Orthodox traditions. Its first recorded mention comes from *The Apostolic Tradition*, by Saint Hippolytus of Rome (ca. 215 AD):

> The Deacons shall then bring the offering to him [the Bishop]; and he, imposing his hand on it, along with all the presbytery, shall give thanks, saying: "The Lord be with you."
>
> And all shall respond, "And with your spirit."
>
> [Bishop] "Hearts aloft!"
>
> [All] "We keep them with the Lord."
>
> [Bishop] "Let us give thanks to the Lord."

---

[65] Cf. Exo. 12:7.

[66] Because the Flesh is eaten and the Blood is drunken under the guise of unleavened bread and wine, we can eat and drink it under obligation, otherwise, it would be a sin according to Lev. 3:17 and Dt. 12:23.

[All] "It is right and just."

This confessional dialogue between the Priest and the People, now belonging as such to a variety of rites, has multiple word arrangements, but all are comprised of an opening blessing, **"The Lord be with you"** for the Latins, and generally the longer **"May the love of God the Father, the grace of the only-begotten Son, and the unity and indwelling of the Holy Spirit be with you, forever"** for the Orthodox Catholics. This opening of the *Sursum corda* echoes Saint Paul's farewell blessing to the Church at Corinth, where he wrote, **"The grace of the Lord Jesus Christ and the love of God and the fellowship of the Holy Spirit be with you all."**[67] This more extended blessing is not needed to be fully repeated in the Novus Ordo Rite, because it was already offered once in the opening of the first movement, and in its current form is closer to the original.

Then, in response, the royal priesthood imparts their blessing on their Priest by saying, **"And with your Spirit."** Just as the change that occurs in the minuet by going from the full orchestra down to a smaller group of instruments gives us the feeling of it being a new composition, so too does this blessing from the Priest that call us to harken back to the opening of the Divine Symphony where he offered us the same blessing, and again before the Gospel was read. Each time this blessing and response blessing signals to the People that there has been a liturgical escalation in the principal matter of Divine Symphony, which is to make Christ Jesus present to His People.

When the Priest raises his hands and implores us, **"Let us lift up our hearts,"** and we agree with him, saying, **"We lift them up to the Lord,"** we put ourselves in union the Prophet Jeremiah, who said, "Let us lift up our hearts as well as our hands toward God in

---

[67] 2 Cor. 13:14.

the Heaven!"[68] It is at this moment at Mass when the People of God incorporate their whole body in the Divine worship by spiritually extending themselves towards the Heavens to place their heart where their treasure is.[69] Saint Cyril of Jerusalem in his twenty-third of twenty-four *Catechetical Lectures* (350 A.D.) wrote of how this periodic phrasing calls us to devote ourselves to the principal matter of the Sacrifice of the Mass:

> After this, the Priest cries out: "Your hearts aloft!" For truly, in the most solemn hour, it behooves us to have our hearts aloft with God, and not below, with the earth and earthly things. It is, then, as if the Priest instructs us in that hour to dismiss all physical cares and domestic anxieties and to have our hearts in Heaven with the benevolent God. Then you answer: "We keep them with the Lord," giving assent to it by the avowal which you make. Let no one come here, then, who could say with his mouth, "We keep them with the Lord," while he is pre-occupied with physical cares."

Then comes the climax of the *Sursum corda* when the Priest extends his hands and proclaims through invitation that the hour for the Holy Eucharist (i.e., the sacrifice of thanksgiving)[70] has now arrived; **"Let us give thanks to the Lord."**[71] This one moment is everything! It is the moment that all the universe patiently waits to begin. It is the melodic key to the angel's morning song. It is why the saints love to pray. It is all that the Christ Mass, Pentecost, and the final coming is. This moment is the spark that ignites the reason why we have faith, why we hope, and why we

---

[68] Lam. 3:41.
[69] Cf. Mt. 6:21.
[70] Cf. CCC. 1360.
[71] Cf. 1 Chr. 16:18; 2 Chr. 20:21, 31; Judith 8:25, Ps. 7:18, 9:2, 56:10, 137:1; Isa. 12:4, 1 Cor. 15:57, 2 Thess. 2:13; Rev. 11:17.

love. This moment opens the door the principal matter of the Divine Symphony, and it is why we respond in a praiseworthy manner, **"It is right and just."** Saint Cyril of Jerusalem continues:

> Then the Priest says, "Let us give thanks to the Lord." Surely, we ought to give thanks for His having called us, unworthy though we are, to so great a grace; for His having reconciled us when we were His enemies; for our having been deemed worthy of the adoption of sons by the Spirit. Then you say, "Worthy and just;" for in giving thanks, we do a worthy thing, and just. But what he did in accounting us worthy of such great benefits was not merely just, but more than just.

It is true. It never seems enough at this moment just to respond, **"It is right and just."** It is as if the People of God are having a spontaneous loss of words about what to say in this awesome moment. They seem to be stunned like Peter was, who in seeing Jesus transfigured on a high mountain and Moses and Elijah appear to them, could only respond, "Lord, it is good that we are here."[72] It also right that the Priest stops us in our tracks from saying something utterly trivial and worldly as Peter went on to say.

To help the People of God express what their heart only yearns to acclaim, in the older rites and in Eucharistic Prayers II and IV of the Novus Ordo, the Priest most fittingly builds upon their response and acclaims us why it indeed is right and just that they give thanks to the Lord:

> It is truly right and just, our duty and our salvation, always and everywhere to give you thanks, Father most holy, through your beloved Son, Jesus Christ, your Word through whom you made all things, whom you sent as our Savior and Redeemer, incarnate by the Holy Spirit and born of the Virgin. Fulfilling your will and gaining for you a holy people, he

---

[72] Mt. 17:4.

stretched out his hands as he endured his Passion, so as to break the bonds of death and manifest the resurrection (Eucharistic Prayer II).

Although this prayer may vary with important Feasts, it primarily consists of three confessions: 1) A Confession why it is good to give thanks; 2) A type of Creedal confession of our belief in the Father, Son, and Holy Spirit and in their work of creation; and 3) A Confession about our belief in the salvific work of Jesus Christ. In the older rites, such as the Missa Cantata of the Dominicans and the Tridentine Mass, the prayer following the *Sursum corda* are only concerned with the first two parts, but adds an ending that leads directly into the 'the Santus'; **"Which the Angels and Archangels, the Cherubim also and the Seraphim do praise: who cease not daily to cry out, with one voice saying ..."** The Liturgy of the Byzantine Rite confesses all four parts of this prayer, and adds another by giving thanks to God for the liturgy itself:

It is proper and just to sing hymns to You, to bless You, to praise You, to give thanks to You, to worship You in every place of Your dominion; for You are God ineffable, inconceivable, invisible, incomprehensible, ever existing, and eternally the same; You, and Your only-begotten Son, and Your Holy Spirit; You brought us forth from nothingness into being, and when we had fallen raised us up again and left nothing undone until You brought us to Heaven and bestowed upon us Your Kingdom to come.

For all this, we give thanks to You, and to Your only-begotten Son, and to Your Holy Spirit, for all that we know and that we do not know, the manifest and the hidden benefits bestowed upon us.

We thank You also for this liturgy, which You have willed to accept from our hands, even though there stand before You thousands of archangels, tens of thousands of angels, Cherubim and Seraphim, six-winged, many-eyed, soaring aloft on their wings.

At the end of this prayer, the Priest joins his hands together and concludes the Preface with the people, singing, or saying 'the Sanctus' aloud, **"Holy, Holy, Holy Lord God of hosts.**[73] **Heaven and Earth are full of your glory. Hosanna in the highest.**[74] **Blessed is He who comes in the name of the Lord. Hosanna in the highest."**[75] Whereas, the People whose faith is so pure and innocent, who could not fittingly express, or trust in their Priest to most perfectly express, why it is right and just to give thanks to God, now are so filled with joy at the Priest's acclamation that they can only respond by singing or saying aloud what Isaiah confessed, "In the year King Uzziah died, I saw the Lord seated on a high and lofty throne, with the train of his garment filling the temple. Seraphim were stationed above; each of them had six wings: with two they covered their faces, with two they covered their feet, and with two they hovered. One cried out to the other: "Holy, holy, holy is the LORD of hosts! All the Earth is filled with his glory!"[76]

This repeating language in the prayer prefacing 'the Sanctus' and in Isaiah's confession about there being Angels, Archangels, Cherubim and Seraphim around the Lord throne, and how what is happening in Heaven affects what happens on Earth is also found in John's witness in the book of *Revelation*:

---

[73] Cf. Rev. 4:8.
[74] Cf. Isa. 6:3.
[75] Cf. Psa. 118:26; Mt. 21:9; Mk. 11:9-10.
[76] Isa. 6:1-3.

At once I was caught up in spirit. A throne was there in Heaven, and on the throne sat one whose appearance sparkled like jasper and carnelian. Around the throne was a halo as brilliant as an emerald. Surrounding the throne, I saw twenty-four other thrones on which twenty-four elders sat, dressed in white garments and with gold crowns on their heads.

From the throne came flashes of lightning, rumblings, and peals of thunder. Seven flaming torches burned in front of the throne, which are the seven spirits of God. In front of the throne was something that resembled a sea of glass like crystal. In the center and around the throne, there were four living creatures covered with eyes in front and in back. The first creature resembled a lion, the second was like a calf, the third had a face like that of a human being, and the fourth looked like an eagle in flight.

The four living creatures, each of them with six wings, were covered with eyes inside and out. Day and night they do not stop exclaiming: "Holy, holy, holy is the Lord God Almighty, who was, and who is, and who is to come."

Whenever the living creatures give glory and honor and thanks to the one who sits on the throne, who lives forever and ever, the twenty-four elders fall down before the one who sits on the throne and worship him, who lives forever and ever. They throw down their crowns before the throne, exclaiming: "Worthy are you, Lord our God, to receive glory and honor and power, for you created all things; because of your will they came to be and were created.[77]

---

[77] Rev. 4:2-11.

This singular and beautiful melody of the second section of this minuet is thirsting so desperately to lead us into this one Divine reality; that when our eyes fall upon the sanctuary where the Priest, *in Persona Christi*, is standing, we are beholding the throne of our Lord where He is about to come in His Real Presence. The drama of this melody is that what we see now at this moment at the Sacrifice of the Mass is what Isaiah saw, it is greater than what Peter, James, and John witnessed at the Transfiguration, and it is what John of *Revelation* beheld.

I do not agree with Saint John Vianney's saying that "If we really understood the Mass, we would die of joy," because no one would dare attend the Mass if death with a smile were the pinnacle of its realization. Far too extreme is dying of joy, but if we were to just remove our sandals after confessing 'the Sanctus,' as Moses did when we came before the Burning Bush, we might be substantially closer to be doing what is proper and right at this moment. For, through our sense alone, if we are attentive to the changes in form, the liturgy informs us that 'the Sanctus' is an extraordinary confession. We remain standing to confess it, and then (for us Latins) fall to our knees for the first time immediately after having said it. As for why we kneel, rather than stand as they do in the East, Joseph Ratzinger had this to say about the origin and purpose of falling to our knees during the Divine Symphony:

> When a man kneels, he lowers himself, but his eyes still look forward and upward, as when he stands, toward the One who faces him. To kneel is to be oriented toward the One who looks upon us and toward whom we try to look, as the epistle to the Hebrews says, "looking to Jesus, the pioneer, and perfecter of our faith."[78] [79] . . . In the Hebrew of the Old Testament, the verb *barak*, "to kneel," is cognate with the

---

[78] Heb. 12:2; cf. 3:1.
[79] *The Spirt of the Liturgy*, 197.

word *berek*, "knee." The Hebrews regarded the knees as a symbol of strength; to bend the knees is, therefore, to bend our strength before the living God, and acknowledgment of the fact that all that we are we receive from Him.[80]

Robert Cardinal Sarah connects our kneeling with God's silent presence:

When they want to look at God, Oriental peoples kneel down and prostrate themselves, with their face to the ground, as a sign of voluntary humiliation and respectful reverence. Without a strong desire to be rid of oneself, to make oneself small in the presence of the Eternal, no conversation with God is possible. Similarly, without mastery of one's own silence, no encounter with the other person is possible. If we remain ourselves, we are full of noise, conceit, and anger.[81]

Just as old as any of the other prayers and confessions in the Divine Symphony, not only is 'the Sanctus' rooted deeply in sacred Scripture and tradition, it also filled with allegory:

While we shout the triple acclamation of, "Holy, holy, holy," it is nevertheless understood that there is only one lordship, one power, and one divinity. It will be remembered that the prophet Isaiah saw the Lord on an exalted throne in mists of incense with the angelic powers surrounding Him crying out, "Holy, holy, holy is the Lord of hosts."[82] And "one of the seraphim flew to [the prophet], having in his hand a live coal which he had taken with the tongs from the altar. And he touched my mouth with it, and said: 'Behold, this has touched your lips; your iniquity is taken away, and your sin is purged.'"[83]

---

[80] *The Spirit of the Liturgy*, 191.
[81] *The Power of Silence*, 63.
[82] Isa. 6:1-4.
[83] Isa. 6:6-7.

The details in this passage from Isaiah are interpreted allegorically as the Priest at the Holy Table holding in his hands the spiritual coal, the Eucharistic Christ, sanctifying and purifying those who partake. For Christ has penetrated the Heavens,[84] and we have Him as an advocate before the Father, the one who forgives all our sins.[85]

The Faithful also shout, "Hosanna in the highest. Blessed is he who comes in the name of the Lord." The Hebrew word hosanna, found only in *Psalm* 118:25 in the Old Testament, consists of the imperative hosanna, "save," followed by the participle na, meaning "we beseech." Thus *Psalm* 118:25 is translated, "Save now, I pray, O Lord." The word hosanna is, therefore, a cry for help from those in distress. In the Liturgy, hosanna is an admission of the wretched position our sins have placed us in; and at the same time, it is an exclamation of trust that our God can save us if we beseech Him.

The phrase, "Hosanna in the highest!" might mean that we are calling upon all the angelic hosts "in the highest" realms of Heaven to assist us in crying to the Lord, "Save us now!" Or "in the highest" may mean, "to the utmost," so that we are imploring God to perfect His salvation in us. Blessed be Jesus Christ who is about to come to us in the Eucharist to save all who partake![86]

Regarding this testimony in the Gospels, they are all in harmony with each other in saying that Jesus was met by a sizeable crowd who had given Him a king's greeting and blessing. *Luke* is the only one that departs from recording that this crowd said *Hosanna* as He entered Jerusalem. The message being conveyed here with this greeting is that as they pay homage to the

---

[84] Heb. 4:14.
[85] 1 Jn. 2:1-2.
[86] *Understanding the Orthodox Liturgy: A Guide for Participating in the Liturgy of St. John Chrysostom.* 90.

Messiah-King, they are also simultaneously crying out to Him for help. *Psalm* 118:25-26 is the source of this high greeting, and it is still used today in the liturgy of Jewish Seder (Passover) ritual. "In the highest," refers to the Most High - Help, I pray in the name of YHWH. *Mark's* "Blessed is he who comes in the name of the Lord! Blessed is the Kingdom of our father David that is to come!" is similar to a passage found in the *Didache*, "Let grace come and let this world pass away. Hosanna to the God of David. If any man be holy, let him come! If any man be not, let him repent: Maranatha ["Our Lord! Come!"], Amen."[87]

The Synoptic Gospels also insist that the crowd participated in welcoming the Messiah King into Jerusalem by spreading their cloaks on the ground before Him. It is worthy to note here that an Israelite's cloak was probably the most valuable possession on his or her body. Therefore, this great sacrifice of their most valuable possession expressed total dependence on God, and was immediately woven into their cry for help!

The Lucan narrative departs from the oral tradition which says, 'many in the crowd joined in by spreading branches from trees onto the ground', but *John* disagrees with all of them by informing us that these branches were not even from the native Judean trees, as *Matthew* and *Mark* posit, but they were actually *palm* branches that had to be imported from afar.[88] *John* may be making a symbolic statement here by linking palm branches with victory because, during the second Jewish revolt, the symbol of palm branches was used on coins.

It is, indeed, a beautiful irony, that the first time Christ Jesus heard many people cry out to Him, saying "Hosanna to the Son of David; blessed is he who comes in the name of the Lord; Hosanna in the highest,"[89] was near the Feast of the Passover when He

---

87 Cf. 10:6.
88 Cf. 2 Macc. 10:7.
89 Mt. 21:9.

processed into Jerusalem, and a very large crowd laid their cloaks and palm branches before Him. We, the People of God gathered at memorial sacrifice, are the perfect fulfillment of those earlier People. For, many of them did not even know who He was, and those who did thought he was just a prophet "from Nazareth in Galilee,"[90] but we Catholics know Him just as Cephas knew Him, as "the Messiah, the Son of the living God."[91] Then, just a few days after they cried out to Him for help, many of these same people joined in with the religious leaders, saying, "Let Him be crucified,"[92] but their death wish became the source of salvation of His People.

Together, these mysteries of Heavenly worship and hopes redeemed is what makes 'the Sanctus' such a powerful prayer, and the reason why in many Catholic dioceses we fall to our knees after we confess it.

THE EUCHARISTIC PRAYERS OR ROMAN CANON OR ANAPHORA

Then the Priest, with his hands extended, echoes that last confession we sang and said aloud together with him, saying:

We give you praise, Father most holy, for you are great and you have fashioned all your works in wisdom and in love. You formed man in your own image and entrusted the whole world to his care, so that in serving you alone, the Creator, he might have dominion over all creatures.

And when through disobedience he had lost your friendship, you did not abandon him to the domain of death. For you came in mercy to the aid of all, so that those who seek might find you. Time and again you offered them covenants and

---

[90] Mt. 20:11.
[91] Mt. 16:16.
[92] Mt. 27.22.

through the prophets taught them to look forward to salvation.

And you so loved the world, Father most holy, that in the fullness of time you sent your Only Begotten Son to be our Savior. Made incarnate by the Holy Spirit and born of the Virgin Mary, He shared our human nature in all things but sin. To the poor, He proclaimed the good news of salvation, to prisoners, freedom, and to the sorrowful of heart, joy. To accomplish your plan, He gave himself up to death, and, rising from the dead, He destroyed death and restored life. And that we might live no longer for ourselves but for Him who died and rose again for us, He sent the Holy Spirit from you, Father, as the first fruits for those who believe, so that, bringing to perfection His work in the world, He might sanctify creation to the full." (Eucharistic Prayer IV).

If you recall from the top of this chapter, in the Jewish Passover Seder Ritual, it is the role of the father to instruct his son and those gathered at the table on why 'this night is different from all other nights.' After the question is asked the father would then declare the presence of the Lord, our God, by explaining to his son how the People of God arrived in Egypt, their maltreatment there, and how the Lord brought them out of their bondage and into a land flowing with milk and honey.[93] At the first New Covenant Seder, the disciples witnessed Jesus, who is in His Father and His Father in Him,[94] fulfill this charge of the Seder when He told His disciples how this night is different from every other night when He pointed to Himself as being the new lamb, new unleavened bread, and His Blood as the new drink.

---

[93] Cf. Deut. 26:5-11.
[94] Cf. Jn. 14:10-11.

Now, the Priest, in the role of Father, and *in Persona Christi*, also fulfills that same charge of the New Covenant Seder ritual by educating us as to how this night is different from every other night. Like the Jewish father at Seder, he too begins with the disgrace of the fall and ends with the glory of our salvation through Christ Jesus.

Therefore, when we hear the Priest's confessional story at this subject of the Liturgy of the Word, we are called at that time to enter the role of being a child sitting at a table with our father and hearing him recount the story of our salvation history before we eat the Passover meal.

Also, inasmuch as it is vital what God did for us, it is equally important to know why God did it. The deeper meaning of the Seder story is that God indeed is with us; that is, God is truly *Immanuel*. The reason why we can believe with confidence the words of the Priest when he says, "**. . . you never cease to gather a People to yourself, so that from the rising of the sun to its setting a pure sacrifice may be offered in your name**" (Eucharistic Prayer III) is because there was never a time when God was not with His People. Indeed, the reason why God never ceases to gather His People is because there was never a time when God was not *Immanuel*. The distinguishing character of God's gathered People is that they too are *Immanuel*, because God is with them,[95] and through this nature, God bestows upon the world all that is good.

Not only by this critical identifying mark can the People of God can be found throughout salvation history, but it also addresses the history behind God's motive for entering the world, which, according to *John* was because, "For God loved the world in this way [*houtos*]:[96] that he gave His only Begotten Son, that

---

[95] Cf. Isa. 7:14; Mt. 1:23.
[96] Often translated "so" or "so much", but the Gk. adverb *houtos* is properly rendering 'in this way', 'thus', see also in Mt. 1:18, Mk. 2:12, etc.

whoever believes in Him should not perish but have eternal life."[97]

What is meant by *hoútos*? It is necessitated that the manner by which God loved the world be more than merely offering His only Begotten Son as a sacrifice for the sins of man. On the contrary, it was not Christ alone that came, but it was also His Church. The coming of the Son into the world marked a fulfillment and shift in the temporal nature of the *ekklesia*, whereby it now became the means for man to participate in the Divine nature; that is, the Body of Christ. Therefore, *hoútos* is God, through His Son and the Church (the Body of Christ) bestowing upon the world all that is good. In other words, He loved the world in this way; that He sent His Son to take on our flesh so that through His Church His People might partake in the Divine nature and have eternal life.

For, it was not enough that Christ Jesus was born of a Virgin, crucified, died and was buried, and it wasn't enough for God to just gather together His People, because those two things alone could not have resolved the primordial questions (e.g. 'who am I?', 'how did I get here?', and 'where am I going?') or have redeemed man from his fallen state. There had to be a means by which man could be born anew and be divinized through his free participation and truly become like God, and there had to be a bridge by which those who died prior to the coming of Christ and His Church could also achieve the same. The relationship between the Son, the Holy Spirit, and the Church is what creates that means and the bridge that stretches throughout eternity; never ceasing to gather together the People of God.

Having received the story of our salvation and why God chose us for His Body, we are now ready for the next part of the

---

[97] Jn. 3:16.

New Covenant Seder ritual; the meal, where we consume the Body and Blood of He whom we are being conformed to.

The Priest then joins his hands and extends them over the offerings and prays 'the Epiclesis' (meaning "invocation upon"). **"Therefore, O Lord, we pray: may this same Holy Spirit graciously sanctify these offering,"** the Priest says as he joins his hands and makes the Sign of the Cross once over the bread and chalice together, saying, **"that they may become the Body and Blood of our Lord Jesus Christ for the celebration of this great mystery which He Himself left us as an eternal covenant"** (Eucharistic Prayer III). Through this prayer, the Priest "implores the power of the Holy Spirit that the gifts offered by human hands be consecrated, that is, become Christ's Body and Blood and that the unblemished sacrificial Victim to be consumed in Communion may be for the salvation of those who will partake of it."[98]

The traditional opposition from Eastern Orthodox liturgists is that the Latins put too much emphasis on 'the Epiclesis' and the words of consecration (**"This is my body . . ."**), and that the Aristotelian categories of substance and accidents, and their strenuous search to find that definite point in which the bread and wine become the Body and Blood of Jesus Christ, have rendered the other subjects of the Divine Symphony as nearly meaningless; and for these reasons, the Latins have felt liberated in changing the other parts liturgy of the Mass at their whim.

This traditional refutation of the Latin Rite belongs to the same family of misunderstandings that even many Western Catholics have about their own Mass. They believe that the Mass consists of a menu of things the People say, things the Priest says, times we stand, and times we kneel. They fail to see the continuity, rhythm, and beauty of the whole composition because they don't have ears to hear the Divine Symphony or eyes

---

[98] *GIRM*, III, 79.

to see the great composition and the great Composer of it all. As I wrote in the Proem, it was this family of People who inspired me to write this book.

Back when I had attended my first Catholic Mass in that January of 2006, my only frame of reference for Christian worship was Protestant. Even though only about twenty minutes had passed by the time Father Toner finished his homily, I had every reason to believe that we were headed towards a conclusion of it all, but the liturgy kept going. They were repeating a Creed, saying more prayers, and then they started kneeling and standing. Then, it appeared as though they were about to have communion. Yet, I didn't see a little tray of soup crackers and disposal cups of grape juice ready to be distributed. I already knew I was in a different sacred space than I had ever been before, but in witnessing my first Liturgy of the Eucharistic, I had to feel somewhat like the Disciples at His last Jewish Passover meal must have felt. That is, inasmuch as it was familiar, it was also completely new and, seemingly, wholly consequential.

Now here comes the climax of the second section of the second movement of the minuet. Heretofore in this section, the melodies and subjects of this smaller arrangement of instruments have been ordered to just one theme; that is, the sacrificial thanksgiving offering to God. All that we have prayed and all that we have confessed has been in obedience of the command to "do this in anemeno of Me."

In perfect fulfillment of that command, the Priest stands *in Persona Christi* at the altar of the sacrifice and the table of the Lord, and immediately escalates the gravity of the moment by briefly announcing the occasion that has caused the Latin Catholics to remain humbled on their knees. He clearly and distinctly confesses to God the Father Almighty, **"For when the hour had come for Him to be glorified by you, Father most holy, having loved His own who were in the world, He loved them to the end:**

and why they were at supper" (Eucharistic Prayer IV). The Priest then takes the bread and, holding it slightly raised above the altar, continues, "**he took bread, blessed and broke it, and gave it to His disciples, saying,**" as he bows slightly, "TAKE THIS, ALL OF YOU, AND EAT OF IT, FOR THIS IS MY BODY, WHICH WILL BE GIVEN UP FOR YOU."

He then shows the now consecrated host to the People of God, places it again on the paten, and then genuflects in adoration.

"**In a similar way,**" he continues as he takes the chalice and, holding it slightly raised above the altar and says, "**taking the chalice with the fruit of the vine, he gave thanks, and give the chalice to his disciples, saying,**" as he bows slightly, "TAKE THIS, ALL OF YOU, AND DRINK FROM IT, FOR THIS IS THE CHALICE OF MY BLOOD, THE BLOOD OF THE NEW AND ETERNAL COVENANT, WHICH WILL BE POURED OUT FOR YOU AND FOR MANY FOR THE FORGIVENESS OF SINS. DO THIS IN MEMORY OF ME."

He then shows the chalice to the People, places it on the corporal, and genuflects in adoration.

If the Priest genuflects most reverently after the sacrificial offerings have been consecrated, the People, in turn, are moved to reject all casualness and reject the death caused by meaningless repetition. For, as often as they have heard these words at every Mass for as long as they have been Catholic, how the Priest reverences the Host truly does affect the People's degree of knowing and believing in the awesomeness and seriousness of what has just taken place. That is, what were bread and wine, have now truly become the Real Presence of Christ Jesus among them. God, speaking through His instrument, perfects the creative act of making His words perform precisely what they propose. Saint Ambrose said it this way:

> Be convinced that this is not what nature has formed, but what the blessing has consecrated. The power of the blessing prevails over that

of nature because by the blessing nature itself is changed. ... Could not Christ's word, which can make from nothing what did not exist, change existing things into what they were into before? It is no less a feat to give things their original nature than to change their nature.[99]

Through the miracle of God making His Words come alive, the principal matter of the Mass, to present the Word of God to His people has been accomplished. For this, every eye that beholds the elevated host and chalice should provoke the soul to simultaneous shudder in fear, be overcome with peace, and scream in heavenly praise.

The Presence of God's Body, Blood, Soul, and Divinity among us through the Holy Eucharist is something we all believe by faith and some by the evidence of private revelations, but the minute details and precision of how it all came to be is just as much of a mystery is how the Virgin became the *Theotokos*. About this mystery, Saint Cyril of Alexandria wrote, "Do not doubt whether this is true, but rather receive the words of the Savior in faith, for since He is the truth, He cannot lie."[100]

In knowing how challenging such a miracle can be for some to accept; the Priest beckons the People to affirm their faith by acclaiming 'the Mystery of Faith.'

This acclamation of the People is a most beautiful announcement of their belief that the Sacrifice of the Mass transcends all the boundaries of space and time. Here at this moment, they are pronouncing their belief in the fact that they are far removed from that which is temporal and worldly, but, instead are truly present in the Holy of Holies with God who sees the crucifixion, death, and resurrection of His Son in His eternal now.

---

[99] St. Ambose, *De myst.* 9, 50; 52: PL 16, 405-407.
[100] St Cyril of Alexandria, *In Luc.* 22, 19: OG 72, 912. CCC 1381.

Just as the Passover Meal, the Agony in the Garden, the Arrest, the Trial, the Sentencing, the Way of the Cross, the Crucifixion, and the Death of our Lord took place all on the same day, so too do we acclaim that we are here kneeling on that same day and witnessing in memorial of the re-presentation of that same sacrifice by responding to the Priest either, **"We proclaim your Death, O Lord, and profess your Resurrection until you come again,"** or **"When we eat this Bread and drink this Cup, we proclaim your Death, O Lord, until you come again,"** or **"Save us, Savior of the world, for by your Cross and Resurrection you have set us free."**

Then, once again, the Priest takes the words of truth offered by the People and expounds upon the Passion, resurrection, and glorious return of Christ Jesus they so humbly acclaimed, by confessing, **"Therefore, O Lord, as we celebrate the memorial of the saving Passion of your Son, His wondrous Resurrection, and Ascension into Heaven, and as we look forward to His second coming, we offer you in thanksgiving this holy and living sacrifice"** (Eucharistic Prayer IV). Through this *Anamnesis* (i.e., memorial) prayer the Church "presents to the Father the offering of His Son which reconciles us with Him."[101]

Having prayed for God to accept our offering in fulfillment of the Passover command, the Church then prays that their offering, which has become the Body and Blood of His Son, may now be their food for divinization and union with their Creator; that what they eat, they will become like, saying through the Priest, **"Look, we pray, upon the oblation of your Church and, recognizing the sacrificial Victim by whose death you willed to reconcile us to yourself, grant that we, who are nourished by the Body and**

---

[101] CCC. 1354.

Blood of your Son and filled with his Holy Spirit, may become one body, one spirit in Christ"[102] (Eucharistic Prayer IV).

Still elevating our acclamation that this memorial of the Sacrifice of our Lord is taking place within the eternal now of Lord, in communion with all the People that He has gathered across the ages, next the Priest offers a prayer of intercession for the eternal happiness of the whole Church in Heaven and on Earth, the living, and the dead; together "with the pastors of the Church, the Pope, the diocesan bishop, his presbyterium and his Deacons, and all the bishops of the whole world together with their Churches."[103]

After ending the intercessory prayer in the name of Christ our Lord, the Priest then takes the chalice and the paten with the host and, raising both, he says, **"Through Him, and with Him, and in Him, O God, almighty Father, in the unity of the Holy Spirit, all glory and honor is yours, for ever and ever."** This confession from Saint Paul's letter to the Church in Rome is a doxology to the Holy Trinity that,[104] in the context of the moment, expresses all that which the Priest holds in his hands; that all of creation is completely dependent on God for all that it is and all that it ever will be. By acclaiming **"Amen,"** the People of God close the second section of the minuet, in the same manner, they closed the first.

Even though this second section of the minuet was narrowly focused on the subject of the memorial of the Passover sacrifice, the degree of activity in the Liturgy may give the impression to some that 'the Eucharistic Prayers' are more transactional in nature than they are relational. I do agree, without fault, that the Eucharistic language of offering, sacrifice, and giving, is very transactional, and I posit that the language and activities are

---

[102] 1 Cor. 10:16-17.
[103] CCC. 1354.
[104] Cf. Rom. 11:36.

transactional because the admirable exchange, itself was a high-est of all transactions, by which God became man so that man might become like God, and this transaction is the first fruit of the principal matter of the Divine Symphony.

Along with the memorial sacrifice being transitional in activity, I find that 'the Eucharistic prayers' also have the charac-ter of being the par excellence expression of theology, because they perfectly propose the lived experience of faith seeking un-derstanding.

It is common to view the Scriptures as being a handmaid or one of the many sources by which we do theology, but the Bible alone cannot be a theological expression, because it is neither systematic, academic, rigorous, nor dogmatic; nor does the Scrip-tures respond to our direct questions or define theological terms. That is the wrong way to think of *theo-logia*, which simply means 'study of God.' On the contrary, doing theology is primar-ily living and participating in the story of God, through which we grow in the knowledge of Him through that experience. The irony of sacred Scripture is that it is full of stories of people who actually took the time to experience life with God; people who failed and got back up with His help. Inasmuch as all faithful Jews devoted themselves to the study of Scripture, they also under-stood that to cooperate with God they had to leave the book and go and be used by Him. Then, from that experience, lived out over centuries, comes the questions, answer, systems, rigor, dogma, and academia.

The reason why the Sacrifice of the Mass is the perfect ex-pression of what Saint Anselm called *fides quaeren intellectum* ["faith seeking understanding"], is because it is the story of God in the form of a sacrament that we are commanded as His People to receive and to participate in. Indeed, receiving God through His story is something Jews have always known; we see that in their Scriptures and in their rituals; most especially in the Passover Seder ritual. The Catholic Church fulfills this same calling, to make God present to His People by telling them His story and commanding them to participate in it; most perfectly through the liturgy of the memorial sacrifice.

The *Ite, Missa est* is the fulfillment of the Jesus' commission to His disciples to "Go therefore and make disciples of all nations, baptizing them in the name of the Father and of the Son and of the Holy Spirit, teaching them to observe all that I have commanded you; and lo, I am with you always, to the close of the age."[105] For, it is through the sacrament of Baptism that we receive the indwelling of the Holy Spirit and membership into His Church (the Body of Christ), and it is through that Church that the magisterium and their participants (i.e., Priests and Deacons) teach all of the receive the commands of Jesus that have been revealed in the heritage of faith contained in sacred Scripture and Tradition,[106] and it is through the Holy Eucharist, consecrated at Mass, that our Lord remains with us always, to the close of this age.

For these reasons, after this second section of the minuet has concluded, the Catholic should be left knowing that they have just participated in the Divine drama through which God is courting His People to be reconciled to Him through the Sacrifice of Christ Jesus His Son on the Cross. It is a true saying that the path to sainthood is tied to the path of experiencing God in our life with the Cross.

THE COMMUNION RITE

Now, the orchestra returns to the minuet for this final section of the third movement in the Divine Symphony. Whenever

---

[105] Mt. 28:19-20.
[106] Cf. CCC. 891.

I see the two lines of People processing up to receive the Holy Eucharist, the first thing I think of is a minuet dance with Christ and His Bride; its choreography of dancers (His People) lined up; its bowing and curtseys as they do, and as we, at minimum, ought to also do before we receive our King; then returning to the line again as we process to take the chalice or return to our pew to kneel for prayer. To be sure, 'the Communion Rite' is a dance, but it is the most intimate and fulfilling nuptial dance in the entire universe. There is nothing like it on our side of existence.

With the primary character of the Divine Symphony being a memorial and a sacrifice, and its principal matter being making God present to His People, the central purpose the Mass comes to be fulfilled in 'the Communion Rite', which is to make God's People like Him; that is, to be divinized – given the gift of true life – the life for which those who cooperate with God were created for. It is for this reason that the Church teaches that the Lord invites and urges us to receive Him in the sacrament of the Eucharist, saying "Truly, I say to you, unless you eat the flesh of the Son of man and drink His blood, you have no life in you."[107] For, outside of the Triune God living within us, we are apart from Him, and that separation is, truly, eternal death.

With this clear purpose in mind, the Priest sets down the chalice and the paten, and then joins his hands to say, **"At the Savior's command and formed by Divine teaching,[108] we dare to say,"** and as he extends his hands outward and, together with the People of God, continues, **"Our Father, who art in Heaven, hallowed be thy name; thy kingdom come, thy will be done on Earth as it is in Heaven. Give us this day our daily bread, and forgive us our trespasses, as we forgive those who trespass against us; and lead us not into temptation, but deliver us from evil."[109]**

---

[107] Jn. 6:53; Cf. CCC. 1384.
[108] Cf. Mt. 6:9.
[109] Mt. 6:9-13.

It is a peculiar liturgical innovation, only found among some of the participants in the Novus Ordo Rite, that even though in all the previous moments where the Church called the Priest to stand in the orans posture (arms outstretched – *in modum Crucifixi*), the People did not imitate him, but now they do. Before, it would have been a chore for some of them just to get their hands out of their pockets, but now they move to imitate the Priest in extending their arms outward.

Using the orans posture for private and non-liturgical prayer is one those things that seems to just pour out of our human nature. In every ancient religion; monotheistic or polytheistic, the adherents of that practice can be found crying out to their God with their arms outstretched. Even some of the tombs in the catacombs show someone in the orans posture supplicating God on behalf of the deceased.

Yet, within the context of the memorial sacrifice, the private use of the orans posture amongst the laity was foreign until the Catholic charismatic renewal that sprung up, beginning in the late 1960's. In fact, it was not until the Sacred Congregation for Rites issued *De musica sacra et sacra liturgia* (*Instruction on Sacred Music and Sacred Liturgy*) on September 3, 1958, that the People of God were even given permission to pray 'the Pater Noster' in unison with the Priest:

> Since the Pater Noster is a fitting, and ancient prayer of preparation for Communion, the entire congregation may recite this prayer in union with the Priest in low Masses; the Amen at the end is to be said by all. This is to be done only in Latin, never in the vernacular.[110]

The private use of the orans posture during their charismatic renewal gatherings eventually found their way into the Divine

---

[110] *De musica sacra et sacra liturgia*, 32.

Symphony and grew in great popularity only due to a grave mis-understanding of what the Sacrifice of the Mass is, of what 'the Our Father' prayer is, and of what the Priest is doing when he is offering this outward sign of intercessory prayer for the People. Rather than imitate the Deacon (assuming he is not also pretend-ing to the be a Priest and praying with his arms extended), they have voluntarily decided to obstruct the system of outward signs by praying as the Priest prays or, even worse, hold hands to-gether. The Vatican's 1997 *Instruction on Certain Questions Re-garding the Collaboration of the Non-Ordained Faithful in the Sacred Ministry of the Priest* has this to say about this grave innovation to the liturgy:

> To promote the proper identity (of various roles) in this area, those abuses which are contrary to the provisions of Canon 907 are to be eradicated. In Eucharistic celebrations, Deacons and non-ordained members of the faithful may not pronounce prayers (e.g., especially the Eucharistic prayer, with its concluding doxology) or any other parts of the liturgy reserved to the celebrant Priest. Neither may Deacons or non-ordained members of the faithful use gestures or actions which are proper to the same Priest celebrant. It is a grave abuse for any member of the non-ordained faithful to "quasi-preside" at the Mass while leaving only minimal participation to the Priest which is neces-sary to secure validity.[111]

To protect and to secure the validity of the memorial sacri-fice, the Deacon and the People must not offer and any sign, ges-ture, or word, which would give the indication that they are con-celebrating the Mass with the Priest, that they are also *in Persona Christi*, that they are interceding for the People with him, or that they are also consecrating the offerings. Principally, that means that the People must be attentively and participatively silent in

---

[111] *ICP Practical Provisions* 6, 2.

God through all of their language of word and body, except when the Church has given them the words to speak and the bodily language to express. For, it should not be a novel idea that we should trust that the liturgy is for our benefit and that any obstruction to it can be spiritually harmful to many.

In the instant case, the People join the Priest in praying 'the Our Father' because it disposes them to receive all that the memorial sacrifice proposes. In praying 'the Our Father,' the Priest and the People together summarily and succinctly pray and confess all that they have prayed for and confessed up this moment. Tertullian had this to write about the fullness and breadth of this prayer: "The Lord's prayer truly is a summary of the whole Gospel."[112] Similarly, Saint Thomas Aquinas agreed with Saint Augustine of Hippo, in writing, "The Lord's Prayer is most perfect, because, as Augustine says (*ad Probam Ep.* cxxx, 12), "if we pray rightly and fittingly, we can say nothing else but what is contained in this prayer of our Lord."[113] As 'the Our Father' expresses the fullest hope the ministry of Christ Jesus, so too does the Divine Symphony.

The mystery and paradox of this prayer are most clearly evident when we pray it while our eyes are fixed on the Crucifix. Beginning with, **"Our Father, who art in Heaven, hallowed be thy name; thy kingdom come, thy will be done on Earth as it is in Heaven,"**[114] we confess what we have already confessed in opening of 'the Creed'; what Your People have always said the *Shema*, and what Your first commandment obliges us to believe. Moreover, Lord, by this confession we believe and know that we are nothing in comparison to You O' Lord. We are small, and You are entirely other in Heaven. Our name is nothing, but Your name is

---

[112] *De oratione*, 1.
[113] S.T., II-II, Q. 83, art. 9.
[114] Mt. 6:9-10.

holy, holy, holy. Our word has the power to do nothing, but Your creative word can do all things on Earth and in Heaven.

In petitioning, **"Give us this day our daily bread,"**[115] we beg that Your word be may true again, O Lord, and in our total dependence on Your mercy, we pray that You will sustain our life daily by giving us the bread of life. We beg of You to sustain us as You sustained Your People in the desert. Give us, Eternal Father, not a storehouse full of this bread, that we might grow boastful and independent, but give us the manna we need daily so that we might always be reminded that we are Your children.

In praying, **"And forgive us our debts, as we also have forgiven our debtors; and lead us not into temptation, but deliver us from evil,"**[116] just as we asked of You in 'the Confiteor' and our Priest has interceded for us through this memorial sacrifice, forgives us of all our sins and all of our offenses against You, our neighbor, and ourselves, so that we might worthily receive our daily bread; Your Son Jesus Christ. O' Lord, hand us not over to the tests of Satan, as You handed over Job, but, rather, order our steps and may Your Word be a light to our path according to the purpose for which You created us so that we might always cooperate with Your holy will, and never with the Evil one.

As he has done times before in the liturgy, with his arms remaining outstretched, the Priest takes up our humble cry into his office of intercession, saying, **"Deliver us, Lord, we pray, from every evil, graciously grant peace in our days, that, by the help of your mercy, we may be always free from sin and safe from all distress, as we await the blessed hope and the coming of our Savior, Jesus Christ."** To which the People offer a doxology in glory of their Eternal Father's name, the coming of His reign, and the power of His saving will; signifying their total dependence upon

---

[115] Mt. 6:11.
[116] Mt. 6:12-13.

Him and their total rejection of the false kingdom of the Evil One, saying, **"For the kingdom, the power and the glory are yours now and forever."**

That concluding acclamation of 'the *Pater Noster*' is rooted in the public blessing that King David offered the Lord in testimony that all gold, silver, bronze, iron, and precious stones that the People offered to build the Temple came from God:

> Blessed are you, Lord, God of Israel our Father, from eternity to eternity. Yours, Lord, are greatness and power, glory, victory, and splendor. For all in Heaven and on Earth is yours; yours, Lord, is kingship; you are exalted as head over all. Riches and glory are from you, and you have dominion over all. In your hand are power and might; it is yours to give greatness and strength to all. Therefore, our God, we give you thanks, and we praise the majesty of your name.[117]

It should not be glossed over the fact that beginning with 'the Our Father,' the central theme of this final section of the third movement is medicinal. That is, the repeating note in our prayers is a cry for the food that heals us from sin. In the instant case, we prayed **"forgive us our trespasses, as we forgive those who trespass against us; and lead us not into temptation, but deliver us from evil;"** to which the Priest interceded, **"that, by the help of your mercy, we may be always free from sin and safe from all distress."**

The reason why there is such a very heavy emphasis on sin in this section is so that the People will be properly disposed in every way to receive the remedy for their chronic condition. For Christ, Himself said, "those who are well have no need of a physician, but those who are sick; I have not come to call this righteous, but sinners to repentance."[118] True to His every word,

---

[117] 1 Chr. 29:10-13.
[118] Lk. 5:31-32.

Christ Jesus is Present at the memorial sacrifice and comes as the Holy Eucharist to be the great Physician to give peace and healing to those who have fallen into the maladies of this transitory life.

If Catholics were attentive to the prayers and confessions in this section of the liturgy, I would hear far fewer complaints from them about how their Priest never talks about sin in his homily, because the primary and oft-repeated subject of this section is sin and its remedy. In fact, the condition of sin is being prayed and confessed about so much so that if you do not know you are sick now, perhaps you should reanalyze why you have come to this specialized hospital for sinners.

The words of consecration contain medicinal themes, such as **"my Body which will be given up for you,"** and **"my Blood ... poured out for you and for many for the forgiveness of sin."** Only a heavenly hospital could undertake the work of such a Divine transfusion, through which the patient is healed of sin by incorporated their body into a whole new Body and receiving all new Blood. For, as the Catholic Church teaches, there can be no remedy of our grave condition without at the same time cleansing us from past sins and preserving us from future sins:

> For as often as we eat this bread and drink the cup, we proclaim the death of the Lord. If we proclaim the Lord's death, we proclaim the forgiveness of sins. If, as often as His blood is poured out, it is poured for the forgiveness of sins, I should always receive it, so that it may always forgive my sins. Because I always sin, I should also have a remedy."[119]

The Church is the only hospital that is in the sole business to treat the chronic disease of sin, and the remedies that God has

---

[119] CCC. 1392, St. Ambrose, *De Sacr.* 4, 6, 28: PL 16, 446; cf. 1 Cor. 11:26.

given Her to heal His People's wounded condition are the Sacraments; chiefly Baptism which once and immediately heals us of the effects of the original sin and unites us with our permanent family Physician; Penance and Reconciliation which immediately absolves and heals us from the guilt of sin incurred after Baptism; the Anointing of the Sick which immediately confers upon the infirm the special grace of healing and comfort, and the Holy Eucharist which immediately grants the increase in grace for freedom from light daily faults,[120] remission of punishments,[121] preservation from mortal sins,[122] restraint of concupiscence,[123] growth of the virtues,[124] sanctification in Christ,[125] and more.

Yet, just as no competent physician of this world would dare to operate on a person who is in no condition to survive surgery, neither does the Catholic Church offer the Holy Eucharist to those who are attached to grave sins, because the effects of the medicinal increase in grace it confers may only harm them more. On the contrary, just as a competent physician would work to make their patient healthy enough to recover from surgery, so too does the Church prepare the penitent to have peace, rather than to be condemned by Christ Jesus coming to dwell within them.

For, what person who is doing evil would invite the police into their home? What student asks his instructor to watch him cheat on an exam? What man invites his wife to the home of his mistress? Everyone would agree that if you are doing wrong, and do not want to be judged for it, it would be ill-advised to expose yourself to your judge. The same holds true for receiving the

---

[120] *Denzinger*, 43rd Edition [hereafter 'DZ'], 1638, 1740, 3375.
[121] *DZ*, 1020.
[122] *DZ* 846, 1322, 1638, 3375.
[123] *DZ*, 3375.
[124] *DZ*, 846.
[125] *DZ*, 4010.

Holy Eucharist unworthily, and for this reason, Saint Paul wrote the Church at Corinth:

> Therefore, whoever eats the bread or drinks the cup of the Lord unworthily will have to answer for the Body and Blood of the Lord. A person should examine himself, and so eat the bread and drink the cup. For anyone who eats and drinks without discerning the Body, eats and drinks judgment on himself. That is why many among you are ill and infirm, and a considerable number are dying. If we discerned ourselves, we would not be under judgment; but since we are judged by [the] Lord, we are being disciplined so that we may not be condemned along with the world. Therefore, my brothers, when you come together to eat, wait for one another. If anyone is hungry, he should eat at home, so that your meetings may not result in judgment. The other matters I shall set in order when I come.

A person who is concerned about their eternal destination would take heed to these words of the Apostle and never feel pressured to get into the communion procession to receive Christ Jesus within them. Regardless of social pressure, this is not the time to 'do what Catholics do' or to be seeing 'being Catholic,' because those who receive the Holy Eucharist unworthily may complicate matters for themselves and may go from bad to worse, and from sick to death. This admonition is true; receive the Holy Eucharist, but receive it not if you are not fit to have your Judge come to dwell inside of your home.

Continuing his prayers of intercession for Christ to give His peace to remedy our chronic condition, the Priest, standing in the orans posture, begs the Lord to be true to His word, saying aloud, **"Lord Jesus Christ, who said to your Apostles: Peace I leave you, my peace I give you;**[126] **look not on our sins, but on the faith of**

---

[126] Jn 14:27.

your Church, and graciously grant Her peace and unity in accordance with your will." He then joins his hands back together, and offers the doxology, "Who live and reign forever and ever."[127] To which the People respond, "Amen."

In petitioning the Lord to heal us, not according to our sins, but, rather, according to the "faith of your Church," for a second time in the same prayer the Priest asks Christ Jesus to be true to His word and heal us as He healed the hemorrhaging woman, who had the faith, hope, and audacity to reach out and touch the fringe of His garment. Seeing her, He said, "Take heart, daughter; your faith has made you well."[128] The Priest is begging Jesus to heal us not according to our sins, but, rather, according to the faith that compels us to call Him Lord, just as He healed the blind men who believed in Him. He touched their eyes and said, "According to your faith be it done to you." And their eyes were opened."[129]

If more of the world had the faith, hope, and audacity of these souls, the communion line would stretch on for miles with People processing up to the Lord, believing that He was going to heal them of their chronic condition by the touch of the Holy Eucharist on their tongue.

Although his words are brief, the prayer that Jesus Christ "graciously grant Her [His Church] peace and unity in accordance with your will," is loaded with theological implications unique to Catholicism. Namely, that we believe that the Church Herself has a nature that we call the Body of Christ, and through Her nature, the People of God are incorporated into that Body and, thereby, reconciled and bought into unity with God the Father.

---

[127] Ps. 146:10.
[128] Mt. 9:22.
[129] Mt. 9:29-30.

Traditionally, the preferred method by which the Church has sought to express how it is that the People are incorporated into the nature and the Body of Christ is through the reality of the Sacrament of the Eucharist and its words of consecration found in the Gospels and *First Corinthians*,[130] This, the Church has found, is the central mystery in explaining God's love for His people and our participation in His Divine nature.

Again, in his letter to the Church at Corinth St. Paul was admonishing them about their factions and divisions, which were being raised by the failure of some to discern the Body and Blood faithfully. He warned against this failure, stating, "For anyone who eats and drinks without discerning the body, eats and drinks judgment on himself. This is why many among you are ill and infirm, and a considerable number are dying."[131] Similarly, about fifty years after St. Paul's letter, St. Ignatius of Antioch wrote to the Church at Smyrna concerning the same:

> But consider those who are of a different opinion from us, as to what concerns the grace of Jesus Christ which is come unto us, how contrary they are to the design of God. They have no regard to charity, no care of the widow, the fatherless, and the oppressed; of the bond or free, of the hungry or thirsty. They abstain from the Eucharist, and from the public offices; because they confess not the Eucharist to be the flesh of our Savior Jesus Christ; which suffered for our sins, and which the Father of His goodness, raised again from the dead. And for this cause contradicting the gift of God, they die in their disputes; but much better would it be for them to receive it, that they might one day rise through it. It will, therefore, become you to abstain from such persons, and not to speak with them neither in private nor in public.

---

[130] Mt. 26:20-30; Mk. 14:17-26; Lk. 22:14-23; Jn. 6:45-59, 13:21-30; 1 Cor. 11:23-29.
[131] 1 Cor. 11:29-30.

For Ignatius, the denial of the confession that the Holy Eucharist is the flesh of Jesus Christ was an anathema, and those who abstain from the Holy Eucharist because they deny it should, themselves, be abstained from by Christians.

The writer of the *Gospel of John* wrote similarly to Ss. Paul and Ignatius in saying that God's reason for sending His Son is because He loved the world, and that "everyone who believes in Him might not perish but might have eternal life."[132] Later *John* connects the belief in the Holy Eucharist; that it truly is the Flesh and Blood of the risen Lord, to eternal life.[133] That is, we are not only called to believe that the Christ has come, but also that He comes as the Holy Eucharist, and will come again at the end of time. "Whoever believes in Him will not be condemned, but whoever does not believe has already been condemned, because he has not believed in the name of the only Son of God."[134]

It is the Holy Eucharist that unites the Baptized into the whole Mystical Body of Christ in the Universal Church (i.e. the Church Militant, the Church Suffering, and the Church Triumphant) and across the span of space and time, precisely because it is that uniquely unifying reality of the condescending nature of the Church which is eternal and preexists the purely human nature of the Church that is becoming one with Christ through their communion; that is, through their restored participation in the Divine nature with Him.

The consistent teaching of this union between man and the Bodily Incarnate Son of God, through His Eucharistic Body, and facilitated by the ecclesial Body (the Church) is, per Benoit-

---

[132] Jn. 3:16.
[133] Cf. Jn. 6:45-51.
[134] Jn. 3:18.

Dominique, "well-established in patristic writings"[135] and the Fathers were intent on making it more explicit.

Enclosed within the covenantal economy of the nature of the Church is the sign of bread representing the Presence of God among the gathering of His People. In *John 6*, Jesus points to this Covenantal sign of God's Presence through the auspices of bread, saying, "Truly, truly, I say to you, it was not Moses who gave you the bread from Heaven; my Father gives you the true bread from Heaven. For the bread of God is that which comes down from Heaven, and gives life to the world." The multitude of people who were fed by the multiplication of loaves and fishes said to Him, "Lord, give us this bread always." Jesus said to them, "I am the bread of life . . . "[136] In this dialogue, Jesus identifies Himself with the miracle of bread that rained down from Heaven that

---

[135] de La Soujeole, Benoit-Dominique. *Introduction to the Mystery of the Church*: The Catholic University of American Press. Washington D.C. 2014. 79. Print. In this section on the Data of Tradition Benoit-Dominique bundles three of the five principal apostolic Fathers (St. Clement of Alexandria, St. Ignatius of Antioch, and the author of the *Didache*) and demonstrates how these early testimonies offered an overall vision how the Incarnate Word of God makes Himself present in the Eucharist and, thereby, unites in Himself all of the faithful as the Church. For St. Irenaeus to be united to Christ is to be in His Church and, thereby, under the authority of the Bishops of the Church, who are the successor of the Apostles. To break away from the Apostolic teaching and preaching is to break away from the Body of Christ. For St. Athanasius, man can only be saved by being incorporated into Christ and, thereby, becoming a son of God. "This movement of man's salvation," according to Benoit-Dominique is, "remains entirely dependent upon the first movement of the Incarnation." According to St. Cyprian, the Church is a people who are united to the Holy Trinity and to the bishop, who is the shepherd. ". . . . whoever is not with the bishop is not in the Church." Moving forward into the periods of St. Hilary, St. John Chrysostom, St. Cyril of Alexandria, St. Augustine, St. Thomas Aquinas, *De Ecclesia*, Pope Pius XII's *Mystici Corporis Christi*, and *Lumen Gentium*, Benoit-Dominique presents data to the demonstrate the consistency of the belief, through the ages of the Church, that the Baptized are union with the Body of Christ, but development in regards to the precision in how we might classify the distinction between the physical Body of Christ and the body of man.
[136] Jn. 6:32-35.

promised to sustain the material life of the Israelites in the desert[137] and points to the coming of a new bread that promises an eternal in the world to come.

The five thousand who were fed through the multiplication of five barley loaves and two fishes can be viewed as a typology narrative for the story of when David approached the priest Ahim'elich and demanded "five loaves of bread, or whatever is here" for his men to eat, but being that there was no common bread for the priest to share, he gave David the only bread he had, which was the holy bread (show bread), "the bread of the Presence,"[138] which the Lord always commanded to be set on the table in front of the Ark of the Covenant.[139] The fulfillment of the Presence bread in the New Covenant is in Jesus Christ. Whereas the Presence bread was so called because it sat before the Presence of God through the Ark of the Covenant, the Holy Eucharist is the actual Real Presence of the Body of God the Son.

This new bread is also called "flesh"[140] and, thereby, contains the fulfillment of God's love and Presence among His People that He decreed to Moses, "And the Lord said to Moses, "I have heard the murmuring of the sons of Israel; say to them, "At twilight you shall eat flesh, and in the morning you shall be filled with bread; then you shall know that I am the Lord your God."[141]

God who created the body of man, saves man through the Body of His Incarnate Son. The Body of Christ is the Presence of God on Earth, which was prefigured by the bread of the Presence and is now fulfilled as the bread of the Holy Eucharist that comes down from Heaven. For his part, man participates in this saving work of God by becoming members of the Body of Christ

---

[137] Cf. Exo. 16.

[138] 1 Sam. 21:6.

[139] Cf. Exo. 25:30; Lev. 24:4-9; 1 Chron. 9:32; 1 Kings 7:48. 2 Chron. 4:19, 13:11.

[140] Jn. 6:51.

[141] Exo. 16:12.

through Baptism and by receiving the Body of Christ through the Holy Sacrament of the Altar.

Despite the limitations that space and time impose, and man's ability to fully know God's work, Scripture and Tradition attest to the truth that throughout salvation history, Christ Jesus has identified His Body with both the body of those He has come to save and with sacraments of their salvation. Thereby, through His death and resurrection, He lovingly binds Himself to all those who have died in Him so that they might partake in the nature of God and in His Resurrected Body that He deigned to share with them.

Now, for the second time in this movement and for the fourth time in the Divine Symphony, the Priest signs that the liturgy has just escalated in its principal matter to make Christ Jesus present to His People. He turns towards them, extending and then joining his hands, and says, **"The peace of the Lord be with you always."**

The Church added the words **"peace"** and **"always"** to the Priest signal because they belong to the essential properties of the gift that the People are about to receive. In regard to the Eucharistic property of 'peace,' through healing our wounds, the Holy Eucharist grants us that same peace which was prophesized by Isaiah, who wrote, "But He was wounded because of our sins, crushed because of our iniquities. He bore the chastisement that made us whole, and by His bruises, we were healed."[142] Similarly, but not the same, our own cross that we have been carrying to Calvary has been accompanied by hardship. The sins of the world and the price we have paid for falling into temptation have beaten us down, punished us, and left us with scars, but Christ took up our wounds in His own, paid the price for our sins, and healed us all in His resurrection. Therefore, in saying, **"The**

---

[142] Isa. 53:5.

peace of the Lord be with you always," the Priest echoes the Apostle who wrote to the Church at Corinth, "For since death came through a human being, the resurrection of the dead also came through a human being. For just as in Adam all die, so too in Christ shall all be brought to life,"[143] and it is through the seven Sacraments of birth, increase, healing, and mission, administered through the Church, that we participate in that new state of being.[144]

Further, in adding the word **"peace"** the Church is also reminding us that in the Holy Eucharist, Christ Jesus is truly present among us, and whenever we know and believe that Jesus is present, there is truly peace in that space. The Church is asking Her children to recall all the instances recorded in sacred Scripture where Jesus oftentimes prefaced His sudden presence among His disciples with the words, "Do not be afraid," and "Peace be with you." While it is terribly unfortunate that God appearing as bread and wine is not as shocking to our senses of fear and anxiety as it ought to be, with these words, the Church is calling us into the awe and reverence of God truly coming among us.

The essential Eucharistic property of **"always"** or 'eternally,' calls us to remember the command and promise that God attached to the gift that we are about to receive. The command to celebrate the Passover sacrificial memorial is perpetual;[145] meaning, that until Christ returns at the end of the age, from rising of the sun to its setting, a pure sacrifice will always be offered in the name of God. Attached to the fulfillment of this command is the promised blessing, that those who perpetually celebrate the sacrifice and eat the Lamb of God, will be passed over and spared from death. In the Christian context, that means that

---

[143] 1 Cor. 15:21-22.
[144] CCC. 1210.
[145] Cf. Exo. 12:14.

God's abiding Presence will remain with those who eat the Body and Blood of Jesus Christ, and they will have eternal life.[146]

In closing with the short period phrasing again, **"And with your spirit,"** the People pray that the promised peace and blessings of the Holy Eucharist also come down and rest upon their Priest.

Then, if appropriate, the Deacon or the Priest asks the People to share the joy of reconciliation that they have received in Christ with their brothers and sisters by offering to **"each other the sign of peace."** The ancient practice of Catholics greeting one another with a *Holy Kiss* or *Kiss of Love* is found in several of the Epistles.[147] Its place in the liturgy, after 'the Eucharistic Prayers' and prior to the distribution of the Holy Eucharist, is attested to by of Saint Justin Martyr in his *First Apology*; writing, "Having ended the prayers, we salute one another with a kiss."[148] Although, it must be stated that in some expressions of the Novus Ordo in the East, 'the Sign of Peace' is exchanged, not before Communion, but before 'the Presentation of the Gifts,[149] which, as I will explain below, is a more Scriptural and meaningful place in the liturgy to position it.

As a sign of unity, the *Holy Kiss*, now called 'the Sign of Peace,' is a fulfillment of our Lord's admonishment, that, "If you are offering your gift at the altar, and there remember that your brother has something against you, leave your gift there before the altar and go; first be reconciled to your brother, and then come offer your gift."[150] The Apostle wrote about the fruits of reconciliation with Christ in this way, "For if while we were enemies we were reconciled to God by the death of His Son, much

---

[146] Cf. Exo. 12:13; Jn. 6:52-57.
[147] Cf. Rom. 16:16; 1 Cor. 16:20; 2 Cor. 13:12; 1 Thess. 5:26; 1 Pet. 5:14.
[148] St. Justin, *Apol.* 1, 65.
[149] Cf. *The Spirit of the Liturgy*, 170.
[150] Mt. 5:23-24.

more, now that we are reconciled, shall we be saved by His life. Not only so, but we also rejoice in God through our Lord Jesus Christ, through whom we have now received our reconciliation."[151] The Elder also admonished that our sacrifice is evil if we do not love our brothers and sisters, writing, "For this is the message which you have heard from the beginning, that we should love one another, and not be like Cain who was the evil one and murdered his brother ... Little children, let us not love in word or speech but in deed and in truth."[152]

In properly connecting the work of our hands with the fruit of our life, the Eastern liturgies position 'the Rite of Peace' prior the Eucharistic Prayers. In the Maronite Rite, the Priest prays in part, **"Enable us to greet one another with a holy kiss, worthy of your holy name,"** and is followed by the Deacon announcing, **"Let each of us give the greeting of peace to our neighbor, with that charity and loyalty which is pleasing to the Lord,"** to which the People respond by offering to each an embracing hand and words of peace. In the Divine Liturgy of Saint John Chrysostom, there is a great deal of kissing. Up to the Rite of Peace, the Priest has already kissed the icon of Christ, the icon of the Theotokos, the holy Gospel Book, the Holy Table, the Hand-Cross, the orarion (the Deacon's and Sub-deacon's vestment), the epigonation, the phelonion (the poncho worn over the Priest's vestments), and the Holy Gifts. Then at 'the Rite of Peace' the Priest kisses all the holy things, and if there are other Priests present, they kiss each other on the shoulder.

Similarly, in the Tridentine Mass, 'the Sign of Peace' is only exchanged among the clergy, but is given by offering to each an embracing hand, and is positioned in the liturgy prior to receiving

---

[151] Rom. 5:10-11.
[152] 1 Jn. 3:11 ... 18.

the Holy Eucharist. This placement signifies the connection between the gift that we must offer with the gift that we are about to receive.

In the Novus Ordo, 'the Sign of Peace,' like the orans posture and holding hands during 'the Our Father', is one of the subjects that can have the danger of falling out of the sacred if the laity is not rightly instructed and protected regarding its prescription. To be sure, 'the Rite of Peace' is not a free-for-all opportunity to meander about the congregation shaking hands with everyone we see. It is not a social hour or a family reunion. If there is truly someone at the Mass whom you need to be reconciled with prior to receiving the Holy Eucharist, then, most certainly, go to that person and let your embracing hand, kiss, or bow be sober and solemn and offer little resemblance to our 'happy-to-see-you' greetings in the world. In 2004, the Congregation for Divine Worship and the Disciple of the Sacrament offered this instruction in *Redemptionis Sacramentum* on certain matters to be observed or to be avoided regarding the Most Holy Eucharist:

> It is appropriate "that each one give the sign of peace only to those who are nearest and in a sober manner." "The Priest may give the sign of peace to the ministers but always remains within the sanctuary, so as not to disturb the celebration. He does likewise if for a just reason he wishes to extend the sign of peace to some few of the faithful." "As regarding the sign to be exchanged, the manner is to be established by the conference of Bishops in accordance with the dispositions and customs of the People," and their acts are subject to the *recognition* of the Apostolic See.[153]

This need for uniformity and protection from error over 'the Rite of Peace' has been necessitated by a nearly two-thousand-

---

[153] *Redemptionis Sacramentum*, 73; Cf. *General Instruction of the Roman Missal*, 154.

year-old history of it being abused and causing Catholics to harm each with it and to arouse suspicions of immorality with the public. In 175 A.D. Saint Athenagoras warned that we should give the most exceptional care to guard our bodies against defilement and corruption, "If anyone kisses a second time because it has given him pleasure, he sins."[154] Twenty years later Saint Clement of Alexandria cautioned, "Love is not proved by a kiss, but by a kindly feeling. But there are those who do nothing but make the Churches resound with a kiss, not having love itself within. For this very thing, the shameless use of a kiss (which should be mystical), causes foul suspicions and evil rumors. The Apostle calls the kiss holy."[155] By 390 A.D. we find in the *Apostolic Constitutions*:

> And let the bishop salute the church, and say, The peace of God be with you all. And let the people answer, And with your spirit; and let the Deacon say to all, Salute one another with the holy kiss. And let the clergy salute the bishop, the men of the laity salute the men, the women the women. And let the children stand at the reading-desk; and let another Deacon stand by them, that they may not be disorderly.[156]

While it may come as a surprise to some that even in the fourth-century there were unruly children at Mass, it should not come as a surprise to anyone that people have always taken advantage of opportunities to corrupt the liturgy; to take what is beautiful and make it ugly; to take what is Divine and make it an occasion for sin and scandal. Therefore, the Bishops, Priests, Deacons, Religious, and the People do a good and holy thing when they fight to keep the Divine Symphony free from disorder.

---

154 Saint Athenagoras, *A Plea for the Christians*, 32.
155 Saint Clement of Alexandra, *The Instructor,* III, 11.
156 *Apostolic Constitution*, VIII, XI.

After 'the Rite of Peace,' the Priest takes the Host and breaks it over the paten. Through this action of 'the Breaking of the Bread' (also called 'the Fraction'), the Church points to the first of two paradoxical mysteries contained in this ritual. The first mystery concerns how Christ Jesus is unified with His People through 'the Breaking of the Bread.'

Evident from the words spoken at the First New Covenant Seder Feast, "And He took bread, and when He had given thanks He broke it and gave it to them, saying, "This is my body which is given for you. Do this in *anemeno* of Me,"[157] and evident from the meal He had with two of His disciples near the town of Emmaus, "When He was at table with them, He took the bread and blessed, and broke it, and gave it to them. And their eyes were opened, and they recognized Him; and He vanished out of their sight,"[158] that at 'the Breaking of the consecrated Bread,' Christ Jesus is truly present among His People, and their consumption of His One Body brings them into loving unity with each other and with Him. Through His Presence and indwelling, together, they become and are becoming the Body of Christ. For this reason, *Luke* continues, after the disciples received the gift of the Holy Spirit, they lived a life which closely resembled the liturgy of the Mass, in devoting "themselves to the apostles' teaching and fellowship, to 'the Breaking of Bread' and the prayers."[159]

Luke then goes on to describe the fruit that came to bear from centering their whole lives liturgically on the Presence of Christ Jesus:

> And fear came upon every soul, and many wonders and signs were done through the apostles. And all who believed were together and had things in common; and they sold their possessions and good and distrusted them to all, as any had need. And day by day, attended the

---

[157] Lk. 22:19.
[158] Lk. 24:30-31.
[159] Acts. 2:42.

temple together and breaking bread in their homes, they partook of food with glad and generous hearts, praising God and having favor with all the People. And the Lord added to their number day by day those who were being saved.[160]

The Apostle also wrote about the paradoxical mystery of how the bread that is broken, also makes the many faithful one body in Christ Jesus:

The bread which we break, is it not a participation in the body of Christ? Because there is one bread, we who are many are one body, for we all partake of the one bread.[161]

Just as we all represent many parts of the same Body of Christ, so too is the broken bread we consume all part of the same Body of Christ. We are not all receiving a different piece of Jesus, according to the size, order, or manner, in which we receive the Host. Instead, we all receive an equal fullness of the same Body, Blood, Soul, and Divinity of Christ.

Immediately after 'the Fraction' comes 'the commingling' when the Priest quietly says, **"May this mingling of the Body and Blood of our Lord Jesus Christ bring eternal life to us who receive it."** Through this prayer, the Church points to the second mystery, which concerns how the Holy Eucharist unifies His People with His Church. Symbolically, the ritual of mingling the Body of Christ with His Blood sings of how God's People, the Body of Christ, were brought into union with Him through the Blood of His Only Begotten Son, shed on the Cross.

Through the symbolism of mixing the Blood of Christ with the Blood of His Sacrifice, the Church also audaciously and truth-

---

[160] Acts 2:43-47.
[161] 1 Cor. 10:16-17.

fully declares Her visible, instrumental, universal, and sacramental role in reconciling God's People to Him through the work His Son:

> "The Church, in Christ, is like a sacrament – a sign and instrument, that is, of communion with God and of unity among all men."[162] The Church's first purpose is to be the sacrament of inner union of men with God. Because men's communion with one another is rooted in that union with God, the Church is also the sacrament of the unity of the human race. In Her, this unity is already begun, since She gathers men "from every nation, from all tribes and peoples and tongues;"[163] at the same time, the Church is the "sign and instrument" of the full realization of the unity yet to come.[164]

In his, *A Biblical Walk Through the Mass*, Dr. Edward Sri highlighted the historical tradition behind 'the commingling' ritual:

> In Rome, the pope had a small particle of the consecrated host called the *fermentum* (leaven) sent to Priests in the city, who placed it in their chalices as a sign of their union with the bishop of Rome.[165]

In the Byzantine Rite, the Priest breaks the Holy Lamb into four parts, saying, **"Broken and distributed is the Lamb of God, broken yet not divided, ever eaten yet never consumed, but sanctifying those who partake thereof,"** and then follows, for the Byzantines and for other Eastern rites, subsequent rituals, such as blessing the warm water, consignation, intinction, commixture and elevation (elevation in the Byzantine Rite precedes 'the Breaking of the Bread'). Regarding the former ritual, Najim and Frazier most importantly noted:

---

[162] *Lumen Gentium*, 1.
[163] Rev. 7:9.
[164] CCC. 775.
[165] Sri, Edward. *A Biblical Walk Through the Mass*. Ascension Press. West Chester, Pennsylvania. 2011. 134.

The dominant symbolism is, of course, Christ's sacrificial death. When the Priest says, "broken but not divided," he means that we don't receive a "piece" of Christ when we consume a "piece" of the Eucharist. Christ is fully present in even the smallest particle or drop of the consecrated gifts. Similarly, when the Priest says, "ever eaten yet never consumed," he means that Christ's body can never be entirely eaten, no matter how many liturgies are celebrated around the world on any Sunday. Like the miracle of the multiplying loaves,[166] there are always "leftovers" regardless of how much is consumed. The Church will never run out of the grace of the Eucharistic Mystery.[167]

Taken together, what the Church offers in these two prayers is a statement of faith about the miracle of the Holy Eucharist. We confess that the Holy Eucharist is food that brings eternal life to those who eat it and that it will always be available for those who desire it. In this way, the Holy Eucharist is unlike anything else on Earth. For example, I have a great affection for chocolate covered pretzels, but in matter and substance, one is never exactly like the other; they are all unique, and as delectable as they taste, they don't give me anything Divine. I also have a great affection for musicals, but if the movie *Grease* were ever to be filmed again, it wouldn't be exactly the same as the first one. The actors would have aged, the filmography would not be exactly the same, and there would be something slightly different about the precision of the dance routines and voice inflections during the songs. Moreover, as much as I deeply enjoy a great musical, they don't offer me anything wholly other to what belongs to this world. On the contrary, the source and summit of the Divine Symphony truly is wholly other than the wonderful things of the

---

[166] Cf. Jn. 6:1-14.
[167] *Understanding the Orthodox Liturgy: A Guide for Participating in the Liturgy of St. John Chrysostom.* 109.

world. For, every time we receive Christ Jesus as the Holy Eucharist, it is the same Christ Jesus. While, from Church to Church the accidents of bread and wine might change, God never changes and is never fully consumed.

Meanwhile, as the Priest is executing 'the Breaking of the Bread,' the People are either repeatedly singing or saying aloud 'the Agnus Dei' (i.e. 'the Lamb of God'):

Lamb of God, you take away the sins of the world,
> **have mercy on us.**
Lamb of God, you take away the sins of the world,
> **have mercy on us.**
Lamb of God, you take away the sins of the world,
> **grant us peace.**

First instituted in the liturgy of the Mass by Saint Pope Sergius I (December 15. 687 – September 8, 701), who also instituted the procession for the feasts of the Nativity, Purification, Annunciation, and the Assumption of the Virgin Mary, 'the Agnus Dei' is a type of confessional supplication, which most beautifully seams all the prayers and confessions of the memorial sacrifice together prior to the People receiving the great blessing. That is, not only is 'the Agnus Dei' in union with the minuet's central theme of dependence on God for everything as the remedy for sin, but it also succinctly abbreviates that identical central theme found in 'the Confiteor', 'the Gloria in Excelsis Deo', 'the Kyrie Eleison', 'the Eucharistic Prayers', and 'the Our Father'. In this way, 'the Agnus Dei' ties all that we have prayed and confessed together, and, thereby, humbly demonstrates that just as God is One, so is His Divine Symphony.

Through our participation in 'the Agnus Dei,' we enter the eternity of God, who is beyond all space and time. That is, while God is hearing us say or sing, **"Lamb of God, you take away the** sins of the world, have mercy on us,"[168] He is also simultaneously hearing the witness of John, who when he saw kinsman approach, acclaimed "Behold, the Lamb of God, who takes away the sin of the world! While God is hearing us say or sing **"Lamb of God, you take away the sins of the world, grant us peace,"** He is simultaneously seeing His People, throughout salvation history, eat the sacrificed Lamb, which is the door to their promised inheritance.

Recognizing his own dependence on God and his own need for the remedy of his chronic condition, after he has 'broken the bread', the Priest quietly prays either, **"Lord Jesus Christ, Son of the living God, who, by the will of the Father and the work of the Holy Spirit, through your Death gave life to the world, free me by this, your most Holy Body and Blood, from all my sins and from every evil; keep me always faithful to your commandments, and never let me be parted from you."** or **"May the receiving of your Body and Blood, Lord Jesus Christ, not bring me to judgement and condemnation, but through your loving mercy be for me protection in mind and body and a healing remedy."** This prayer of the Church should not give the faithful the impression that the efficacy of the Sacrament depends in any way on the state of the Priest's soul. On the contrary, the efficacy of the sacraments does not depend on the work being worked by a human, but, rather, they depend solely on the work of Christ Jesus; that is, the sacraments are *ex opera operato Christi*.

Afterwards, the Priest then genuflects before the altar, takes the host and, holding it slighting elevated above the paten or above the chalice, while facing the People (if not ad orientem),

---

[168] Jn. 1:29.

fulfills the promised hope 'the Agnus Dei', in saying aloud, **"Behold the Lamb of God, behold Him who takes away the sins of the world.**[169] **Blessed are those called to the supper of the Lamb.**[170]**"**

As I knelt that first time in that small bland room with my fellow prisoners, slightly confused, but wholly captivated, as Father Toner elevated a white wafer above an old – in desperate need of being polished - gold-plated chalice, I had no idea that I was bearing witness to what the servant John saw in his Heavenly vision. I did not know that John had heard and seen all of us.

John said he "heard what sounded like the loud voice of a great multitude in Heaven, saying: "Alleluia!" Salvation, glory, and might belong to our God, for true and just are his judgments. He has condemned the great harlot who corrupted the earth with her harlotry. He has avenged on her the blood of his servants."[171] In that eternal and timeless space of God, we were the ones whom John had heard acclaiming King David's words of total dependence on God, **"For the kingdom, the power and the glory are yours now and forever."**[172]

When John wrote that he had heard a voice coming from the throne of God saying, "Praise our God, all you his servants, you who revere Him, small and great,"[173] and then heard "the sound of a great multitude or the sound of rushing water or mighty peace of thunder, as they said, "Alleluia," it was our Priests whom he had heard calling on us to give God our praise and thanksgiving, as we acclaim in the Byzantine Rite, **"May our mouths be filled with Your praise,**[174] **O Lord, so that we may sing of Your**

---

[169] Jn. 1:36.

[170] Rev. 19:9.

[171] Rev. 19:1-2.

[172] Cf. 1 Chr. 29:10-13.

[173] Rev. 19:5.

[174] Cf. Ps. 71:8.

glory, for You have made us worthy to partake of Your Holy, Divine, immoral and life-creating Mysteries. Keep[175] us in your Holiness, so that all the day long[176] we may meditate on Your righteousness.[177] Alleluia, Alleluia, Alleluia!"

After the Angel joined us in acclaiming 'the Agnus Dei', "Blessed are those who have been called to the wedding feast of the Lamb,"[178] John witnessed the image of the Church, the holy People of God in Christ, pure in deed, and then he imitated us by falling down in worship.

Then, the servant saw that same Heavenly vision that we see whenever the Priest elevates the Body of Christ above the chalice holding His Blood; writing

"Then I saw the Heavens opened, and behold, a white horse! He who sat upon it is called Faithful and True, and in righteousness, he judges and makes war. His eyes are like a flame of fire, and on his head are many diadems; he has a name inscribed which no one knows but himself. He is clad in a robe dipped in blood, and the name by which he is called is The Word of God. And the armies of Heaven, arrayed in fine linen, white and pure, followed him on white horses. From his mouth issues a sharp sword with which to smite the nations, and he will rule them with a rod of iron; he will tread the wine press of the fury of the wrath of God the Almighty. On his robe and on his thigh he had a name inscribed, King of kings, and Lord of lords. Then I saw an angel standing in the sun, and with a loud voice he called to all the bird that fly in midheaven, 'come, gather for the great supper of God, to eat the flesh of kings, the flesh of captains, the flesh of mighty men, the flesh of horses and their rides, and the flesh of all men, both free and slave, both small and great."[179]

---

[175] Cf. Ps. 40:11; Isa. 42:6.
[176] Cf, Ps. 71:8
[177] Cf. Phil. 4:8.
[178] Rev. 19:9.
[179] Rev. 19:11-18.

Using such Eucharistic symbols as 'dipped in blood,' 'the sun,' and 'flesh,' John could barely describe this moment at Passover memorial feast, but he knew it was something wholly holy, utterly other to the world, and completely consequential to the salvation of many.

The People of God gathered at the Divine Symphony also share this same expression of hope in fearfully, devoutly, and humbling confessing their belief in the convicting and medicinal properties of the Holy Eucharist; saying **"Lord, I am not worthy that you should enter under my roof, but only say the word, and my soul shall be healed."**[180] As a prayer for worthy reception of the Sacrament, in the older Latin rites, such as the Dominican's Missa Cantata and the Tridentine Mass, this confession of the centurion for his servant is fittingly said three times.

THE COMMUNION FEAST

In all the liturgies of the memorial sacrifice, the Priest is the first to partake in the sacrifice offered at his hands. Prior to consumption in the Novus Ordo, he prays again for own soul, quietly saying respectively before he consumes the Body and Blood of Christ Jesus, **"May the Body of Christ keep me safe for eternal life,"** and **"May the Blood of Christ keep me safe for eternal life."**

Here the minuet courtship dance with the Priest and the People returns. After reverently consuming the Body and Blood of Christ, the Priest then takes the paten or ciborium and approaches those who have gathered to receive their King worthily. He elevates the host slightly and shows it to each of the communicants, while proclaiming, **"Corpus Christi (*the Body of Christ*),"** to which the communicant replies, **"Amen."** The faithful then seal their gift with 'the Sign of the Cross,' before turning to

---

[180] Cf. Mt. 8:8.

receive the Blood of Christ or return to their pew where they will kneel silently in prayer and contemplation.

Upon returning to my knees, it has been my practice to pray silently, "Lord, may this Body, Blood, Soul, and Divinity of your dearly Beloved Son, our Lord Jesus, becoming permanently part of me, and that I die unto Him." I am praying that I may decrease so that God will increase. I then wait in silence and hope that God will hear the prayers of my heart. I had to learn how to make my mind, eyes, and body silent, because it was always too tempting to let my eyes fall from the Crucifix to watch the sheep. Yet, there is grace found when we attend to God's silent presence after we receive Him into us.

> There is nothing littler, meeker, or more silent than Christ present in the Host. This little piece of bread embodies the humility and perfect silence of God, His tenderness and His love for us. If we want to grow and to be filled with the love of God, it is necessary to plant our life firmly on three great realities: the Cross, the Host, and the Virgin: *crux, hostia, et virgo. . . .* These are three mysteries that God gave to the world in order to structure, fructify, and sanctify our interior life and to lead us to Jesus. These three mysteries are to be contemplated in silence.[181]

For this moment the Church has arduously prepared us to receive our Lord worthily, and that internal disposition of reverence, humility, total dependence, and love should compel the body, if physically able, to be an externally visible sign of that ongoing internal conversion. For, how we receive our King says everything about how much we revere, how much we are humbled, how much we depend, and how much we love Him. If more People truly understood the gravity of the human body becoming the indwelling of so Holy a sacrament; thereby, making

---

[181] *The Power of Silence,* 57.

our body itself a type of sacrament, I am convinced that everyone would strip themselves down to a sackcloth, put ashes on their head, and for hours or days lie prostrate in the communion line. Then, finally, they would stand and imitate Moses by taking the shoes off their feet,[182] because they would know that where they stand is Holy ground.

Nevertheless, for the Latins, the Church teaches that communicants should position their body to receive the Body of Christ either kneeling or standing, but if standing, it is recommended that they give due reverence before the reception of the Sacrament." Thus, implying that kneeling is the universal norm and the natural external expression of proper reverence,[183] the Church has given individual Bishop's Conferences, with *recognition of the Apostolic See*, the permission to make either kneeling or standing the norm in their own diocese.

Similarly, while the norm for receiving the Body of Christ is on the tongue, Bishop's Conferences, with *recognition of the Apostolic See*, do have the permission to make reception either on the tongue or in the hand the norm in the dioceses'. Thus, demonstrating that receiving on the tongue is the universal norm and the natural external expression of due reverence, reception by hand comes with the warning that, "special care should be taken to ensure that the host is consumed by the communicant in the presence of the minister, so that no one goes away carrying the Eucharistic species in his hand. If there is a risk of profanation, then Holy Communion should not be given in the hand to the faithful."[184]

In the Eastern rites, the Priest or Deacon stands at the Holy Doors, lifts up the holy chalice, and extends it toward the People,

---

[182] Cf. Exo. 3:5.
[183] *Redemptionis Sacramentum*, 90-91.
[184] *Redemptionis Sacramentum*, 92.

saying "Approach with fear of God and with faith."[185] The faithful then approach the Priest by making 'the Sign of the Cross,' bowing reverently and with fear, and then folding their arms across their chest. The Priest then, with a spoon, takes the consecrated leavened bread, dips it into the chalice (i.e. intinction), and then directly places the Divine Mysteries into the communicant's mouth, while once again connecting the Eucharist with true healing, by saying "The servant of God (name), partakes of the precious, most Holy and pure Body and Blood of our Lord, God, and Savior Jesus Christ for the forgiveness of his/her sins and for life everlasting. Amen." During the reception, the Deacon holds the Discos under the chin of each communicant.

As a remedy for our chronic condition, the Holy Eucharist placed on our tongue by the Priest reminds us of Isaiah's vision of the Holy Mass, when after confessing the 'the Sanctus', "Holy, holy, holy, is the Lord of host; the whole Earth is full of His glory,"[186] one of the seraphim flew near to him with a burning coal that had been taken with tongs from the altar and touched the prophet's mouth with it, saying, "Behold, this has touched your lips, your guilt is taken away, and your sin forgiven. And I heard the voice of the Lord saying, "Whom shall I send, and who will go for us?"[187] As Isaiah heard the call to be sent on mission after he was made pure by the touch sacrament of the altar, so too does the Church say to Her People today, *Ite, Missa est,* after they have received the sacrament of the altar.

In addition to the fruit of the Holy Eucharist augmenting our union with Christ, separating us from sin, committing us to the poor, uniting us with other Christians, the indwelling of all that God is, truly does release in us the gift of healing. The Holy Eucharist is the hope of the Prophet Jeremiah who cried out, "Is

---

[185] Cf. Heb. 10:22.
[186] Isa. 6:3.
[187] Isa. 6:7-8.

there no balm in Gilead, no healer here? Why does new flesh not grow over the wound of the daughter of my people?"[188] It is true to say that when God unites His nature with the nature of His communicant, they become a new creation in Him and take on a new flesh in the Body of Christ.

Again, with the primary character of the Divine Symphony being a memorial and a sacrifice, and its principal matter being to make God present to His People, its central purpose is fulfilled in 'the Communion Rite' by making God's People like Him; that is, to be divinized – given the gift of true life – the life for which those who cooperate with God were created for. "Accordingly, the Son of God became the Son of Man, so that the sons of man, that is, of Adam, might become the sons of God."[189] So uniquely other to our temporal plane, the Holy Eucharist cannot help but to also be so singular and extraordinary, even within the community of the seven other sacraments.

Indeed, there are at least five ways in which the singularity of the Divine Mystery helps to inform us of how its fruits configure us to Christ Jesus as nothing else can come close to.

First, the Holy Eucharist is the only Sacrament and only Presence of the four (i.e., the Holy Eucharist, the written Word, the Priest *in Persona Christ*, and the People at prayer) where an actual transfer of matter occurs. That is, what was heretofore the matter of bread and wine, is now no longer, and what took its place is the Body, Blood, Soul, and Divinity of Christ Jesus. While that particular form of transubstantiation can only occur at Sacrifice of the Mass, it is like what the Apostle described what happens to us when we are reconciled to Christ. He wrote, "Therefore, if anyone is in Christ, he is a new creation; the old has passed away,

---

[188] Jer. 8:22.
[189] Saint Clement of Alexandra, *On the Incarnation of the Word of God and Against the Arians.*

behold, the new has come."[190] That quality of transubstantiation of the bread and wine is the model of conversion that our own lives are meant to undergo through God's grace.

Second, the Holy Eucharist is the only Sacrament and only Presence where there is an actual change from something genuinely dead into something truly alive. That is, the written word of God is not living matter, so to speak, and it will always be what it is. For their part, the Priest and the People are living beings and will remain living, because God is "not the God of the dead, but of the living."[191] Yet, the bread and wine, with no life within them, truly become the living Body and Blood of the person, Christ Jesus. What was dead, is now living. Therefore, if by the power of His word, Christ can change a dead thing into a living being, then how much greater can His word effect His life within His living People?

Third, because when we see the Holy Eucharist, we truly see Christ in the Flesh, it persists as the only Sacrament and only Presence that most clearly reminds us of who Christ actually is. In the Holy Eucharist, we have the blessing to perceive with our senses the Real Presence of Christ. Likewise, if Christ lives within us, so too should our brother, sister, and neighbor see Christ when they see us.

Fourth, the Holy Eucharist is the only Sacrament and only Presence that constitutes the most compelling evidence of Christ Jesus at work in the Universe. In other words, if you want to know whether Jesus Christ actually exists, then come to the Sacrifice of the Mass to see Him for yourself. For this reason, the Holy Eucharist instantly fulfills the faith, hope, and love of every Christian.

---

[190] 2 Cor. 5:17.
[191] Mk. 12:27; Lk. 20:28.

Last, the Holy Eucharist is the only Sacrament and only Presence that is intended to be food for the body and soul. It is indeed good advice that we should not attempt to eat or digest any of the other three Presences of Christ at the Mass, because Father would not be happy at all if you started chewing on his or your brother's or sister's arm. The Sacrament of Baptism does require water, but we are not regenerated by consuming it. Confirmation does require chrism oil, but we not are sealed with the Holy Spirit by consuming it. The Holy Eucharist is different from all the other Sacraments in this regard. For, the efficaciousness of the Holy Eucharist comes by way of eating and drinking it. In this way, it reminds the Christian of their complete dependence on God as the source and sustenance of their life.

These five singularities of the Divine Mystery are all together eschatological in that they compel and direct the People of God to reorient their ultimate hope to the fulfillment of the Holy Eucharist; that is, to the day when Christ will come again to judge the living and the dead. This eschatological property of the Holy Eucharist is evidenced in *John*, where Jesus, knowing that some were having a difficult time accepting His invitation to eat His flesh and drink His blood, connected the Blessed Sacrament with His Ascension, saying, "Does this shock you? Then what if you were to see the Son of man ascending to where He was before?"[192] It is true, beholding the Lord under the guise of bread and wine prepares us to see Him finally in His glory. Moreover, the preparations we make to worthily receive Christ Jesus who comes as the Holy Eucharist, lest judgment falls upon us, inspires and propels us to prepare ourselves for His final coming and final judgment. In this way, both the memorial sacrifice and creation share in the same goal and promote our great hope of being divinized through union with God.

---

[192] Jn. 6:61-62.

The series of events that immediately follow the conclusion of the distribution of Communion can seem to be quite non-liturgical and not belonging to the principal matter of the Mass. For a very long time after my own conversion to the faith, I thought the Priest was washing dishes on the altar. To the contrary, what is transpiring here it another ritual of purification. The first part of this ritual is the consumption and/or reservation of the leftover Body and Blood of Christ Jesus:

> When the distribution of Communion is finished, the Priest himself immediately and completely consumes at the altar any consecrated wine that happens to remain; as for any consecrated hosts that are left, he either consumes them at the altar or carries them to the place designated for the reservation of the Eucharist.[193]

The second part is the collection of fragments and the purification of the Holy vessels:

> Upon returning to the altar, the Priest collects any fragments that may remain. Then, standing at the altar or at the credence table, he purifies the paten or ciborium over the chalice, then purifies the chalice, saying quietly, "Quod ore sumpsimus" (Lord, may I receive), and dries the chalice with a purificator. If the vessels are purified at the altar, they are carried to the credence table by a minister. Nevertheless, it is also permitted, especially if there are several vessels to be purified, to leave them suitably covered on a corporal, either at the altar or at the credence table, and to purify them immediately after Mass following the dismissal of the people.[194]

In the current order of the Novus Ordo Rite, while the Priest is carrying out the purification, he quietly intercedes for himself and for the People, praying, "**What has passed our lips as food, O**

---

[193] *GIRM*, Chapter IV, 163.
[194] Ibid.

Lord, may we possess in purity of heart, that what has been given to us in time may be our healing for eternity." This final prayer of the third movement invokes the three aforementioned senses of food that Jesus' command, "Do this in anemeno of Me," brings to perfection in the Holy Eucharist.

Then the Priest may return to the chair, and, if appropriate, allow a moment for the silent presence of God to enter the sacred space where His People are now most intimately abiding in Him and He in them. Otherwise, a psalm or other canticle of praise or a hymn may be sung.

Then, standing at the altar or at the chair and facing the People (if not ad orientem), with hands joined, the Priest says for the second and final time in the Novus Ordo, **"Let us pray."** All then pray in silence with the Priest for a while, unless silence has already been observed immediately prior to the *oremus*. Then the Priest, with his hands extended, says the Prayer after Communion; to which the People acclaim, **"Amen."**

The Fourth Movement
of
The Divine Symphony

EXORDIUM TO THE CONCLUDING RITES

The name of the Divine Symphony itself, *Ite, Missa est* (Go, it is the dismissal), takes its name from these last words spoken by the Priest in most of the older Latin liturgies. These three words are a summary of the ongoing mission of the Church, which is to instill into the People a sacrificial love for all that God loves, by proclaiming the Word, administering the sacraments, and performing works of charity. The Church teaches that the Divine Symphony is called the "Holy Mass (*Missa*)" because the liturgy in which the mystery of salvation is accomplished concludes with the sending forth (*missio*) of the faithful, so that they may fulfill God's will in their daily lives.

In the classical symphony orchestra, the fourth movement was often composed in Rondo form, which consists of a theme (also called a refrain) that is set at the opening of the piece and followed by an episode. While the same theme will be continually repeated, the musical material of the episode is different from the refrain. Unless the Rondo form is combined with Sonata, it usually will not have much emotional depth, but instead, be focused on presenting a fun and upbeat, rollicking finale.

Typically, no one ever thinks of the dismissal and final blessings in the fourth movement of the Divine Symphony as being rollicking or fun, especially when the announcements preceding the blessings are almost always something about what we have already read in the bulletin and something about donations being needed. Yet, there is in the fourth movement a repeated theme that is calling the faithful to action. Similar to a high school pep rally, where some instigator grabs the microphone and yells at the crowd, "Let's go get'em!" Then, in response, the assembly instantly goes crazy with raucous cheers and chants. In our case, it would be like the Priest saying, "You now have God within you! Now, go and do something great with Him! Go be Christ in the world!"

To be sure, what is rollicking about the finale is that 'the Concluding Rite' proposes to excite us to be in the world what we have become to be through the sacred liturgy. It is calling us to 'be' the Mass in the world. Just as our first brothers and sisters devoted "themselves to the apostles' teaching and fellowship, to 'the Breaking of Bread' and the prayers,"[1] so has the Church throughout the ages called us to this same praxis and devotion, so that, through us, the world might experience the miracle of the Holy Eucharist and become like Christ.

As witnesses of the reality of Divine love being completely unable to contain itself, we ought to be excited, ready, and energized to share with the world what we have just received. For, if we love Jesus Christ, and we have just received Him into our bodies, there is nothing that we should not want to do more than to use our bodies to go and glorify Him. Strengthen by the Holy Eucharist, there is nothing we should not want to do after the

---

[1] Acts. 2:42.

memorial sacrifice than go and be a sacrificial offering; offering the peace of Christ where there is chaos, offering the love of Christ where there is apathy, offering the joy and hope of Christ where there is mourning and despair, offering life in Christ where there is death, and sharing the promises and forgiveness of Christ where there is slavery to the temptations of the world, the flesh, and the Devil.

Therefore, with any brief announcements out of the way, the Priest begins this rollicking call to action by facing the People and extending his hands, says, **"The Lord be with you,"** to which they reply, **"and with your spirit."** As with the previous four times, this periodic phrasing signals to the People that there has been a liturgical escalation in the principal matter of Divine Symphony, which is to make Christ Jesus present to His People. The critical distinction between this blessings and response in the fourth movement is that, now, the People are being called to take that principal matter out the doors of the Church and into the world.

The Priest then blesses the People with 'the Sign of the Cross,' while saying, **"May almighty God bless you, the Father, and the Son, and the Holy Spirit,"** and the People respond, **"Amen."** As the Divine Symphony commenced under the holy sign of our Baptism, so too must it conclude. If in the world, important events are marked with distinguishing signs of opening and closing, and at the end of their sporting events there is always a sign given to the victor, so that the crowd will know the champion; then, how much greater should the sign be that is given to God's People at the end of the memorial sacrifice of His Beloved Son?

If it is a Pontifical Mass, the celebrant receives the miter and, begins with the same periodic phrasing, and then harkens us back to 'the Pater Noster'; reminding us of our complete dependence on God, saying, **"Blessed be the name of the Lord,"** and all replying, **"Now and for ever."** He then adds, **"Our help is in the** name of the Lord," to which the People respond, "Who made Heaven and Earth." If he uses it, the celebrant then receives the pastoral staff and says, "May almighty God bless you," while making 'the Sign of the Cross' over the People three times, he adds, "the Father, and the Son, and the Holy Spirit," and People reply, "Amen."

Then the Deacon, or the Priest himself, with hands joined and facing the People says, "Go forth, the Mass has ended," or "God and announce the Gospel of the Lord," or "Go in peace, glorifying the Lord by your life," or "Go in peace," to which the People reply, "Thanks be to God (*Deo gratias*)." All four of these dismissal blessings echo the same theme of all that has been said in 'the Concluding Rite'; that the People are to go give away to the world all that has been given them in the Sacrifice of the Mass.

These dismal blessings echo many of the dismissal blessings in the older liturgies from the East and West. For example, in the Divine Liturgy of Saint Basil, the Priest dismisses the People by distributing to them the antidoron (an ordinary leavened bread which was blessed during 'the Liturgy of Preparation', but is not consecrated), saying, "May the blessing and the mercy of the Lord be with you." In the Divine Liturgy of Saint Mark, the Priest says, "May God bless, who blesses and sanctifies, who defends and preserves us all through the partaking of His holy mysteries; and who is blessed forever. Amen."

Just as the liturgy leads us to Him who is love,[2] and who was sent to us because the Father loves us,[3] and died for us because love for His People, because love compelled Him,[4] so too are we called to go and be love.[5] A Post-Communion prayer found in the Dominican's Missa Cantata liturgy, says it this way:

---

[2] Cf. 1 Jn. 4:8.
[3] Cf. Jn. 3:16.
[4] Cf. Jn. 15:13.
[5] Cf. Jn. 15:9-13.

Strengthened by the Blessed Sacrament, we humbly beseech You, O Lord, that, helped by the example and merits of the blessed Bishop Cyril, we may be worthy servants of the most holy Mother of Your only-begotten Son.

As was said in 'the Introductory Rite,' the Mass is love, and should we leave the Mass with just this one thing that we have been called to, filled with, and strengthen by the Holy Eucharist to be, we will have fulfilled the Law of love that Christ Jesus issued:

> As the Father has loved me, so have I loved you; abide in my love. If you keep my commandments, you will abide in my love, just as I have kept my Father's commandments and abide in His love. These things I have spoken to you, that my joy may be in you, and your joy may be full. This is my commandment, that you love one another as I have loved you. Greater love has no man than this, that a man law down his life for his friends.[6]

Now, having said all that his Mother has called him to say, the Priest venerates the altar as usual with a kiss, just as he did at the beginning. Then, after making a profound bow with the ministers, he withdraws and returns to the People from whom he came.

---

[6] Jn. 15:9-13.

Made in the USA
Lexington, KY
15 July 2018